MONDAYS
don't have to
SUCK!

How small changes can make a huge difference

One man's unintentional journey
of life-altering self-transformation
DAVE WALKER

Copyright © 2018 by Dave Walker. All rights reserved. No portion of this book may be reproduced mechanically, electronically, or by any other means, including photocopying, without permission of the publisher. It is illegal to copy this book, post it to a website, or distribute it by any other means without permission from the publisher.

ISBN: 978-1-7750633-4-6

Published by Dave Walker, Montreal, Quebec, Canada
www.davewcoachingandstorytelling.com

Edited by Susan Crossman - crossmancommunications.com
Designed by Janet Rouss - getrealbranding.com

Dave's book is a message of hope. Change is possible for everyone. Throughout, I noticed a theme of possibility and potential, which encouraged me to explore my choices and potential. Some books I have read made me feel like I was unable to be as amazing as the author, but his book had a non-threatening, human touch i.e. "I did it. It was not always easy. You can do it too, or not". As I read it, I felt like I was always being offered a choice and a gentle challenge. I also appreciate the seasoning of humour that Dave injects into a very real and challenging aspect of life. Dave is truly relatable, inspiring and vulnerable!

Gail McDonald, Owner Octagon Coaching - octagoncoaching.ca
Past President, ICF (International Coach Federation) Edmonton Chartered Chapter

"Dave, trust that your gifts are received as they are from the right place and a deep rooting in an authentic desire to serve. All of our lights burn brighter from your commitment. You have taken the time to craft such a gift to others – especially a 'male group' that are under served in this regard. Applause!"

Jeff Davidson, Partner and Coach at Deloitte

"I love your storytelling. You share so much and really draw me in as a reader!"

Karen Furneaux, Olympian and World Champion Sprint Kayaker
Author of Strong Beauty: POWER UP the Champion Within
International Speaker www.ipromiseperformance.com

Sharing what I learned and leveraged during what became my life-altering journey of change and transformation to help YOU move farther and faster with yours!

Sharing the good, the bad, the just plain ugly and the great to help YOU make your Life Journey EASYer on yourself!

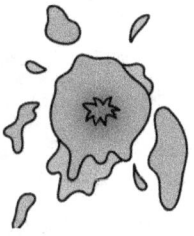

Acknowledgments

I would have to write another book in order to acknowledge all of the people who have helped me put this story together. There were so many of you. My family (especially my sister, Val Walker), and my friends (too many to name, I am truly blessed, but if I had to name just three, it would be you, Deborah Turbitt, and you, Nathalie Duchesnay, and you, Maria Psarra); my clients (thanks for trusting in me and my new calling); my former colleagues (a special thanks to two Partners from my former employer, Adelaide Israelian and Jeff Davidson, who helped me at two crucial junctures of my career); my peers, a whole boat load of fellow coaches (especially my Life Coach, Shawna Corden, and Book Coach and Editor, Susan Crossman); a psychologist (otherwise known as my relationship counselor – thanks, Dr. Janet Takefman); a couple of doctors (especially Dr. Michel Saine); and even a dentist…the list goes on. I also don't want to forget my two beautiful children, Shayne Patrick and Emily Rose, and two very beautiful women, Qita and Monique, who have been, and are still, part of my life. And all this from someone who had shut almost everyone out of his life not that long ago.

Thanks so much for inspiring and empowering me to make and maintain all of the positive changes that I outline in this book. I am so grateful to have you as part of my life. I hope that I have inspired and empowered you in leading better lives, as well…on Mondays, and every other day of the week. ☺

What I have discovered during this most recent journey of mine is that life is an ongoing journey of change, and that there is nothing more powerful than having the support and encouragement of a loving and caring community of family, friends, and co-workers to help make that change happen. To not just make it happen, but to make it EASYer on oneself as it is happening.

I believe that the following quote, which I have affixed to my office wall, sums it up quite nicely.

> "If you want to go fast, go alone.
> If you want to go far, go together"
> — African Proverb

Thank YOU, all!

I am so grateful!

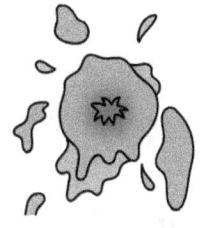

Dedication

This book is dedicated to all of the people who are thinking of making a significant, positive change in their lives – or are in the process of making one – and who could use some encouragement along the way in order to maintain their faith that they are on the right path…i.e. their true and unique path.

This book is also dedicated to all of the people who believe that they have undergone their transition and are now in the process of maintaining the positive changes in their lives. Often, it's EASYer said than done. The majority of people are not able to maintain change. Old habits and mindsets die hard.

And let's not forget the people who believe that life's journey is one of constant change, and who are looking for a way to not only enable the change, but to embrace it, enjoy it, and grow from it.

I am hoping that sharing my story of change with you will inspire and empower you along your journey, YOUR LIFE journey. And I am truly honoured to have the chance to share my story with you! It is my gift to you!

Life's What You Make It[1]

Baby, life's what you make it
Can't escape it
Baby, yesterday's favorite
Don't you hate it
Baby, life's what you make it
Don't back date it
Baby, don't try to shade it
Beauty is naked
Baby, life's what you make it
Celebrate it
Anticipate it
Yesterday's faded
Nothing can change it
Life's what you make it

Song by Talk Talk

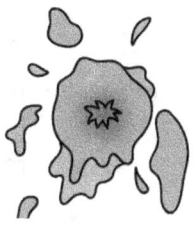

Foreword

What is this Book of Life-Altering Self-Transformation all about?

This book is a story about life-altering self-transformation that did not start off that way. It started with a desire for change and a willingness to get to know myself better…and it took off from there. I took off with it. ☺

Yes, me, myself and I. This story is about me and my LIFE-ALTERING self-transformation on what eventually took place on both the personal and professional fronts. In my case, it came a bit later in the game of life, in my mid-forties, 45 years of age to be exact, but better late than never. As Abraham Lincoln once said:

> *"In the end, it's not the years in your life that count. It's the life in your years."*

I have now positioned myself to get a lot more out of whatever number of years still remain for me. That is very different from where I was not that long ago. I had given up on life. I was just looking forward to the day that I would retire from it, not literally, but from my job at least. I thought that everything would be all fine and dandy when that finally happened. In my case, that was going to be at 55 years of age. Little did I realize at the time, I was probably not going to live that long if I did not make some changes. I had two young children, two children who I love more than life itself.

Actually, this book is two stories. Two stories about two different life journeys that are joined by a fascinating (to me, anyway!) period of transition that I once referred to as a third story of a trilogy..

The first story is about a journey that ended up taking me to a place that I now refer to as my NASTY ZONE and in it, I gave up and let go of my dreams, my career, my friends, my marriage and, finally, myself. The slow slippage inevitably gave way to a dizzying plummet into a state of clinical depression, functional alcoholism, obesity and social isolation. I hit rock bottom. I was stuck at the time and could not imagine a way of moving forward in order to escape that nasty place. I refer to myself during this phase of my journey as OLD Dave (a.k.a. Captain Comfort Zone).

The second story is about a series of catalysts that finally started me moving down a very different life path. The second story is all about gaining momentum by trying, failing and learning from a whole lot of experiences and people that showed up in my life after I had finally decided to move forward. As the momentum built, so did my energy and desire to move even faster and farther. I refer to myself during this phase of my journey as NEWer Dave (a.k.a. Captain Courageous). NEWer Dave – and not NEW Dave – because of my newfound desire to keep changing. Unlike in the past, I learned to enjoy making changes and I especially came to enjoy the positive feelings that started to accompany those changes. I talk now about NEWer Dave because I am hoping that this newer second phase of continuous growth and learning never ends. I want to continue to grow and enjoy life and enjoy all the beautiful people in my life.

Oh, and that third story, the one about the transition…it's been an emotional roller-coaster ride, to be sure, but for the most part, it has been one of the most rewarding and enjoyable times of my life. That's a good thing because, at the time of the writing of this book, I am seven years (and counting) into my transition. If my book coach is right, there may not even be a transition underway. There may not be a third story. This learning and failing and picking myself back up and growing phase actually started seven years ago and may never end until, ultimately, I do. R.I.P. Captain Courageous.

I still sometimes try and take on too much change and overextend myself, which results in what I call a bit of a crash and burn. But, hey, no one is perfect! And despite what I once believed, not every day can be perfect. So, I dust myself off and I take some time to rest and reflect on what has just happened (so hopefully I don't do it again) and then I am right back at it. Back at making my life better, and hopefully the lives of my clients and readers and audiences, as I share my exploits, the good, the bad, the just plain ugly and the great. Failing at it, learning from it and sharing it, one next step at a time.

Is there a secret formula for successfully undertaking self-transformation? If there is, I am all ears. In the meantime, I have come up with one to explore. I share the various components with you as part of this book. I am all about sharing, so it is my pleasure. There is nothing really new in it. It is based on what a lot of people have shared with me, a LOT of people. I have tried a lot of what has been shared with me myself in order to make the theory real. And now I would like to share my lessons learned with you.

I am also sharing some questions of self-discovery since I have found self-awareness and getting to know oneself better (i.e. WHO we are) to be a big part of the formula for success. I'm sharing the stories of my life journey with you. Emotions and all! Yes, a Dude sharing his emotions! It took me a while to share my emotions – which is a big part of the reason that I ended up in my nasty zone – but, as I mentioned previously, better late than never. Oh, and by the way, I am not the only Dude who has had trouble sharing emotions. There are a lot of us out there.

All right already, Dave! Enough background and context. ☺ What is that formula? Oops! (Not only am I a verbal processor, but I am a writing processor as well.) Here you go:

My journey of self-transformation was enabled by what I call the BIG THREE.

1. *Self-Change* (incremental small change steps that help build momentum and confidence, which in turn beget the courage to continue to move forward).

2. *Self-Discovery* (learning about and leveraging what makes us tick, a.k.a. our Unique and Authentic selves. Learning from our successes and failures).

3. *Self-Transformation* (the SHIFTS that come from spending enough TIME working on the previous TWO components of the Big Three).

Oh! and let's not forget that desire to change in the first place.

The Catalyst for change.

Enjoy the read! I truly hope my story helps you in making your life journey better, for you and your loved ones!

CONTENTS

PART 1
SETTING THE STAGE

Chapter 1: A Life-Altering Transformation 3
Chapter 2: "OLD Dave" One Monday, Fall 2009 13
Chapter 3: "NEWer Dave" Monday, December 11, 2017 21
Chapter 4: The BEFORE and AFTER Metrics 29
Chapter 5: My Imperative for Changing My Epitaph 39
Chapter 6: Contemplating a Change to Your Epitaph? 47

PART 2
MY FIRST HALF: CAPTAIN COMFORT ZONE (1965-2008)

Chapter 7: My Search for Success 53
Chapter 8: The Making of Captain Comfort Zone 63

PART 3
A PERIOD OF PAIN IN THE NASTY ZONE (2009-2013)

Chapter 9: Storm Clouds on the Horizon 75
Chapter 10: Hitting the Wall and Getting Stuck 85
Chapter 11: Finding My Fit and a Bit of Self-Confidence 95
Chapter 12: Another Shoe Falls 105
Chapter 13: Grabbing the Oxygen Mask! 115

PART 4
FINDING THE *REAL* ME (2013-2016)

Chapter 14: Finding My FIT-ness Routine 123
Chapter 15: Maintaining My Momentum 133
Chapter 16: Finding My Calling 143
Chapter 17: Firming up My Foundation 153
Chapter 18: Finding the Authentic Me 163
Chapter 19: Finding My Mojo 173
Chapter 20: Having Fun along the Way! 183
Chapter 21: Finding My Heart and My Soul 191
Chapter 22: Finding My Soulmate 201
Chapter 23: Trying Really Hard to Maintain My Balance 213

PART 5
CAPTAIN COURAGEOUS (2017-R.I.P.)

Chapter 24: The Start of My Second Half. Not quite. 223
Chapter 25: Keeping My Courage 233

PART 6
THINKING OF MAKING A CHANGE TO YOUR STORY?

Chapter 26: My Top Three Lessons Learned 243
Chapter 27: My Top 10 Change Enablers 251

PART 7
OUT WITH THE OLD AND IN WITH THE NEWER YOU!

Chapter 28: WHO do you see in the mirror? 269
Resources 277
Endnotes 282

INTRODUCING THE DAVES

NEW (or NEWer) Dave (Or, the Beginning thereof)

Fortunately, I had the wherewithal to snap this selfie at a very special time in my life: December 24, 2014. I was 49 years old. Thanks for the new wardrobe, Santa. Medium, instead of XL.

I will cherish this picture forever – it's one for my time capsule. In the photo I've included here, I thought I was witnessing the "new" me. Turns out it was only the beginning of NEW Dave. It was only the NEW OUTSIDE of me. Things were really going to start picking up momentum when the INSIDE me joined in on the change.

OLD Dave – I have a whole lot of OLD Dave photographs to share, as well. My photo album has at least 15 sad years' worth of them. It's time to start taking more photos of NEWer Dave. Thank goodness for the change. I am grateful. Oh, so grateful.

It is not the mountain we conquer, but ourselves
Sir Edmund Hillary

A journey of a thousand miles begins with a single step.
Lao Tze

PART 1
Setting the Stage

Chapter 1: A Life-Altering Transformation

Life is a giant roller-coaster ride. The thrills and screams, twists and turns, the ups and downs and it's all over way too soon. Enjoy the ride.

Unknown

My life-altering transition! It's been a bit of a roller-coaster ride, actually, so I thought this photograph was appropriate.

In my case, the ride (a.k.a. the journey) was much more pleasant on the way up to my second half ☺ than it had been on the way down during my first half! ☹

Now that I've introduced NEW Dave and OLD Dave, I thought I'd explain why I wrote this book and, more importantly, what's in it for you!

At first glance, it might look as if this story is all about me. I can see how you might get that impression. I do use "me, myself, my, and I" a lot. I've also included a lot of me-related photographs and statistics.

That's not just my ego pushing its way out front. By sharing my story of change with you, I thought I might make it EASYer for you to take away some key learnings to help you on your own journey of change. Books and scholarly journals, and blogs, etc., have a lot to say about what we should be doing to enable positive change in our lives. By contrast, I've tried to make the theory real by trying it all out on myself first, then sharing my lessons learned with you.

And by "my story of change," I mean the story of my life-altering self-transformation; in my case, it was brought on by a mid-life crisis. At least I think it was a mid-life crisis that brought about my desire, or readiness, to change. To find out, I Googled the definition of mid-life crisis:

> *A mid-life crisis is a transition of identity and self-confidence that can occur in middle-aged individuals, typically 45-64 years old. The phenomenon is described as a psychological crisis brought about by events that highlight a person's growing age, inevitable mortality, and possibly shortcomings of accomplishments in life.*

I invite you to keep that definition in mind as you read my story of transition. It definitely seems to fit me and my situation. I was certainly in that age bracket—my mid-forties – and it was a time when I thought I would be winding down my career and gearing up for retirement. My situation had gotten so bad, at one point, that I almost felt like I was retiring from life and not just work. My "inevitable mortality" certainly came into play; specifically, my fear of a premature death. I didn't want to leave my two beautiful children without a father. This was a fear that eventually became one of the key catalysts for making a lot of the changes I made. And don't get me started on how the definition of my "accomplishments in life" changed in both meaning and importance during that period. As far as the transition portion of the definition is concerned (including my newly-adopted modus operandi of making change EASYer on myself), there were no more powerful enablers of my transition than my new-found levels of self-awareness and self-confidence, both of which, for some reason, were not front and centre during what I refer to as the "first half" of my life. They are now!

And, by "share my story," I mean the good, the bad, the ugly, and the great. I don't want to hold anything back. Some of us learn best from success stories; others learn best from horror stories. I have included both in this book. I personally find horror stories more impactful. Sadly for me, but fortunately for you, I have more than a few of them to share. But don't shed any tears for me. Those horror stories are in the past. Most of my stories these days are of the good and great variety, which is pretty cool, considering where I was not all that long ago.

By the way, I'm not just sharing one story with you. I am sharing two. Two stories for the price of one! One is a story of loneliness, darkness, pain and despair. That story, and part of the first half of my book, are about how I built up my comfort zone and ended up getting stuck in it, a pretty nasty place as it turned out (Chapters 7-13). Maybe some of my story will resonate with you? The second story is about growth and connection and meaning, not to mention a lot of fun. It is about how I was able to get myself out of that nasty zone and start moving toward a good place that eventually turned out to be a really great place, most of the time, anyway (Chapters 14-25). If I can do this, then I'm betting you can, too.

Although the outcomes of both stories are very different, they did have a couple of things in common. They both took place over an extended period of time, multiple years in both cases. And I didn't realize what was actually happening in either situation. The changes were so gradual at times that they went by virtually unnoticed, until momentum and the ripple effect of all of the small, incremental changes started to take effect. By gradual changes and ripple effect, I am alluding to how they worked their magic on me both on my way DOWN toward my nasty zone, and on my way back UP toward a more fulfilling life, as well; hence my desire to tell two stories. I built up a lot of momentum on the way down, and I built up a lot of momentum on the way up. After experiencing the results of both negative and positive momentum, and the impact it all had on my personal foundation, I've decided to try to stick to the positive kind of momentum that moves me forward, thank you very much.

The positive momentum, and the ripple effects, not only carried me out of that place of darkness, they continue to carry me to places I've never been before; some pretty cool places, surrounded by some pretty cool, caring and loving people. It took time and effort to get to where I am today. It takes time and effort to stay here. Lots of it! But that time and effort does not have to be painful and negative, it can be energizing and positive, as well. The main thing is, if you think there's more to life than what you're experiencing now, I invite you to take a shortcut to that endpoint through the stories I tell in this book and the questions I provide for self-reflection. I'm rooting for you!

I learned during my journey of self-transformation that there are no cookie-cutter approaches or quick fixes in this process. Each and every one of us is unique. We're each on a unique journey. It takes a strong sense of knowing (or in my case, discovering) who we are in order to align with a path that is the right fit for us. Finding my "who," or, as I like to refer to it, my authentic self, was a key aspect of my self-transformation. This is very much a story of finding ME, of finding Dave.[2]

I hope that my story helps you get to know yourself a little better, too. After all, you're the one in charge of your life journey. The ultimate decision about the path(s) you choose is all yours! This story details how I was able to break free of the confines of my comfort zone; however I've learned that many others are stuck in comfort zones of their own making as well. Some estimates say that includes 98% of the population. Wow! That means a lot of people are missing out on learning to live more fulfilling lives. I would like to share some of my insights in order to help inspire others (i.e. you) to embark upon a positive journey of change, or, if you've already embarked upon one, to maintain it, or, better yet, to pick up your pace of change. It isn't that I have all the answers, not by any stretch. But I have gathered up what I consider to be some pretty good questions, many that sparked a huge improvement in my quality of life. I would feel really happy if they helped you, too.

Although this is my story, there is nothing I did, and nothing I learned, that can't be used by others. All of the approaches and tools I explored and leveraged (and I tried a lot of them) were ones that others had used before me to enable and maintain change. I didn't come up with anything new. I didn't reinvent the wheel. It was all a matter of choosing the tools that fit me. That meant exploring a lot of them. Trying them. Failing at them. Learning from them.

To that end, I would like to share what I've learned with you. You see, I realize now that I set off on my journey of change pretty much all by myself, with little structure or guidance. I fumbled my way forward, and it took me a long time to get to where I am today. I am hoping that sharing my story and lessons learned with you will allow you to go farther and faster than I did. Farther and faster than you believe possible.

In Chapter 26, I share my "Top Three" lessons learned. What can I say? I'm a big fan of the "Power of Three." In Chapter 27, I share a list of the "Top 10" change enablers that helped me both make and maintain my changes. Like David Letterman, this Dave also likes "Top 10" lists. And what about the last chapter, Chapter 28? Well, that chapter is all about you and the changes you might like to make to your story. The story of your life. What are they? And, more importantly, what's stopping you from changing?

If there's one thing I learned very early on in my journey, one thing I hope you take away after reading this book, it's the importance of making change EASYer on yourself. "Making change EASYer on myself" became my modus operandi, the enabling strategy of my transition. It was the one question I always asked myself: How can I make this next change EASYer on myself? If there is only one thing you take away from this book, I hope it's that one concept: the practice – or better yet, the habit – of always asking what you can do to make your desired change(s) EASYer on yourself.

Before I share with you my "Top Three" lessons learned and my "Top 10" list of change enablers later in the book, I'm going to provide a quick summary of what I learned about making change at the end of each and every chapter. More specifically, what I learned from making that change and how I made that change EASYer on myself ☺ (or not ☹). And, since this book is not just about me, I will also ask YOU what you're doing to make your journey of change EASYer on yourself ☺ (or not ☹) and give you a question or two for you to reflect on.

- Enjoy the story!
- Enjoy the stories!
- Enjoy your journey of change!

SO, WHAT DID I LEARN?

How did I make change EASYer on myself ☺ (or not ☹)? Spoiler Alert

I still haven't figured out how to always love Mondays or the other days of the week. I tried often during my seven-year journey of change, but I haven't yet been able to pull it off. And I've tried all kinds of ways of making things EASYer on myself, but I still can't make it happen all of the time. I can't yet make every day great. Ironically, that quest for perfection and nirvana and a state of constant bliss ended up holding me back from embarking upon the second half of my journey. It was giving up on that goal, one I now believe is unattainable, that allowed me to finally move on.

So, if you're looking for a book that will allow you to live a perfect life, day in and day out, then you might want to make it EASYer on yourself and stop reading this book right now. Maybe return it to the store for a refund. Hey, I'll refund the cost of the book to you if you feel misled by the title.

But, if you're looking to make a positive change in your life, and you're ready to put in the time and effort to make it happen, then I encourage you to read on. Although I haven't reached nirvana, and I don't experience a great day, each and every day, I still can't believe how far I have come. Although the car on my roller-coaster still feels like it's heading downhill from time to time, it happens ever more rarely. And you know what? That's good enough for me. More than good enough. The changes I've made in my life have already had a hugely positive impact on my life. I'll leave the quest for perfection and nirvana and other stressful quests to others. I'm too busy having fun and spending time, including Mondays, doing what I love with the people I love. Not every day, but most of them, and that's a lot more days than before. How cool is that? Hats off to me for making change EASYer on myself! ☺

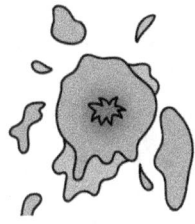

That was all about me. What about YOU?

What are you doing to make your journey of change EASYer on yourself? ☺ (or not ☹)?

Are you ready to make a change? If so, what is your catalyst for change?

- Job got you down?
- Recent divorce?
- Living paycheque to paycheque?
- Is there a toxic situation or person in your life?
- Are you struggling to start up a business for the first time?
- Has parenthood got you a bit stressed?
- Maybe you can't remember what your life partner looks like?
- Mid-life crisis?
- Quarter-life crisis?
- Feeling weighed down by debt?
- Are there people, or is there a person, in your entourage who is draining your energy?
- Feeling like S**T more often that not?
- Feeling pretty good most of the time but looking to take things to the next level?
- You don't want to die prematurely?
- Are you coasting to the finish line of life?

INSERT YOUR Catalyst:

_____

_____

and DESIRED CHANGE:

_____

_____

How will you feel after making that change?

_____

_____

_____

How sure are you that you want to feel this way?

- Well, what's stopping YOU?

Take the time to write it down. Even if you don't want to. It really works to start processing the change when you do this.

_____

_____

_____

_____

_____

_____

_____

_____

_____

_____

_____

Chapter 2: "OLD Dave"
One Monday, Fall 2009

Life's what you make it. Can't escape it.
"*Life's What You Make It*" by Talk Talk

This is a picture of my favourite hidden corner at my favourite food court. One of my favourite hang-outs. More like Monday morning hide-out! Is it Monday again already? This sucks! Big time! I HATE MONDAYS! Holy S**T! How did I end up here?

Dear Diary: Montreal. Monday, Sometime in the Fall of 2009.

5:30 a.m. F**k. It's Monday. I gotta get up. I'm feeling blah. The booze from the past five days has worn off. I should be thankful hangovers are a thing of the past. That's one of the positive aspects of my body adapting to me drinking four-to-six bottles of wine and 12-to-18 bottles of beer a week. So far, my body restricts me to drinking five days a week, Wednesday to Sunday. Five days with a buzz on is all my body will allow. I've tried unsuccessfully to push it to six, but my body just can't handle that much booze, and so it does not let me tank up every day of the week.

I have quite the routine going. From Wednesday to Friday, I get up around 5:30 a.m. and go to work. I arrive home at night and pour my first drink after my children are in bed. I get my buzz going and leverage the accompanying energy boost (a result of a nice big sugar rush) to squeeze in a couple of hours of work before midnight.

On Saturdays and Sundays, I can't seem to summon the energy to move. Once errands I can't put off are done, and child-related activities are complete, I retreat to the den or basement to read newspapers, watch football…or hockey…or movies, lots and lots of movies. I even pay my six-year-old son 25 cents to make sure I never have an empty beer bottle in my hand. Wow. What a role model for a dad!

The Monday and Tuesday schedules are much like what happens from Wednesday to Friday. But I can't drink on Mondays or Tuesdays. My body just can't do it. So here I am. It's Monday, a day when many people find it tough to get out of bed anyway, and I'm coming off my five-day binge. And guess what? No booze to help you today, buddy!

10:00 a.m. S**t. Meeting with my new performance coach. I'm realizing that something isn't right. Really not right. This has actually been coming on for a while now. I can't pretend any longer. I'm in a meeting with my new performance coach who's been assigned to help me get out of the funk I'm in. I'm facing changes after 13 years of steady career progression with the firm, during which time I thought I was heading in the right direction. He tells me I have to get out of my comfort zone. Just once would be a good start, he assures me.

Start networking and meeting new people, try new types of projects, etc. Oh, and sales (for which I now have specific annual targets) is all about relationship-building and would be good for me, he says. Yeah, right. Even hearing the word "sales" makes me want to crawl under a table. But I stay in my chair, my eyes transfixed on his face... he keeps talking and talking and talking about the role and my goals, performance expectations and career path.

It's like his words are going in one ear and out the other as I stare at him, and I think, "What can I do? Look for another job? Start another career?" Now that's a scary prospect. Besides, I'm comfortable here. I'm part of the furniture here. My very specific and narrow area of management consulting expertise has been developed and honed over years. I can't just turn on a dime and learn a different set of skills. I'm no longer a young consultant with lots of time to learn new things. Other people are so much more knowledgeable than I am in these other areas. The thought of selling turns me off, as well. I've been delivering projects for the past dozen years, not selling them. I'm not cut out for that. I've grown into a role that doesn't suit me, but I'm too scared to do anything about it. Even thinking of trying something else terrifies me. So, I try not to think of something else. I try not to think of anything else.

Maybe I can ride this out. A Freedom 55 retirement plan might do the trick. A Canadian life insurance company coined that phrase to inspire people to save money for retirement. Why make changes to my life today when all I have to do is wait for everything to work itself out? That's only a little over 10 years away. My wife and I have no debt and two good incomes. Totally doable. I can start crossing the days off on the calendar and, before you know it, everything will be okay.

If I do decide to leave, my wife has reminded me – often – of the importance of having another job lined up before I go, so there's no disruption in our cash flow, no negative impact on our net worth. I don't think there's a role in another organization that would have a comparable salary. I am actually pretty sure there's not. The bottom line is, I don't believe that there is a future for me in my current role, but I am too scared to do anything about it. Oh, yes, and no booze today, buddy! I hate Mondays! Freedom 55, where are you?

11:00 a.m. Time for my "depression lunch." I feel so alone. I feel so drained, that even getting back to my office is a chore. Sometimes I have trouble breathing. It's like a pain in my gut. I can't tell you how many times I've crashed on the couch at home to read the newspaper or stare at the wall. But I can't crash on my couch because I'm at work. Thankfully, it's time for my preferred workday non-booze-induced escape: my "depression lunch." Time to go hide in the food court near my office. I have a secret spot where no one can find me. I used to limit my lunch breaks to under an hour but, over time, that has somehow morphed into two hours. I'll go grab something to eat. Reading the paper takes my mind off my misery. I hope I'm not missed at the office…

Keeping thoughts of my problems at bay all the time is hard work. Sometimes my mind wanders…I can't help it. Sometimes doubts surface and anxiety takes up residence in my mind. It's hard to describe my feelings – probably because I don't like feeling them. I would rather ignore them and hope they go away on their own. I feel lost, hopeless. They say misery likes company, but I prefer to suffer alone. Oh, yes, and no booze till Wednesday! Did I mention I hate Mondays?

Note to self: I might want to cut down on the fast foods. I stepped on the scale the other night and weighed in at 240 pounds. That's 30 on the BMI scale, which means I'm obese. I'm not surprised. I just can't get myself to exercise, no matter what I try. I feel so isolated, but I don't want to talk to anybody about anything. How did I get here? Oops! No thinking! I don't want to think too much. My lunch is getting cold. I gotta go. I gotta eat. I gotta forget. Let's see, what's new in the world of sports?

6:00 p.m. Home again. It's a wonder I manage to get through the day, especially on Mondays. That's where coffee comes in. Lots of it. A couple of pots a day usually do the trick. That gets enough caffeine flowing through my veins to get me through the day and back home.

If it were any day, other than a Monday or a Tuesday, back home would mean back in front of my first glass of wine. It's the craziest thing. It will be nearing 8:00 p.m. and I've just put my two young children to bed. Time for a couple of hours of work. I'm exhausted. Even the thought of working is a turn-off, but I know that the booze will kick in – and in short order. Once I'm a little over half-way through my first glass of wine, like magic, I'll be completely energized. It works like a charm.

After that bit of work, there's no better way to NOT think of anything else than to go hide in my basement and listen to music and continue to drink alcohol. So, I listen to my tunes for a couple of hours, alone in the dark basement, a full glass in my hand, before going to bed to try to get some sleep. And by "try to get some sleep," I mean just that. Try sleeping after drinking a bottle and a half of wine and two pots of coffee. Not easy. Not easy waking up the next morning either; in my case, waking up in a set of sheets that are soaking wet from night sweats. I've never had night sweats before. Sometimes I have to wring out my pillowcase! At least my wife's side of the bed is dry.

But not tonight, no booze on a Monday night to take my mind off my miseries. I will have to settle for some TV time in order to escape all my scary thoughts. I guess I should be grateful my body still allows me my caffeine fix seven days a week. Yuk. Wednesday, where are you? I miss you! I miss my booze buzz. Did I say I hate Mondays?

SO, WHAT DID I LEARN?

How did I make change EASYer on myself ☺ (or not ☹)?

When I look back at this chapter of my life, there are two words that come to mind, and those words are Escape and Isolation. I just wanted to escape from all of my problems, and the way I did that was through alcohol, movies, TV shows, newspapers, depression lunches, etc. The various methods of escape I tried all resulted in isolation.

I ended up isolating myself from everyone ☹ and I mean everyone ☹ including myself and my feelings. The only exceptions were my children. The worse things got, the more isolated I became, which in turn made me feel even more helpless, depressed and alone, which made me feel even more stuck. Stuck and lost and scared. Escaping. Avoiding my feelings. Isolating myself. Silencing myself. Talk about NOT making change EASYer on myself ☹!

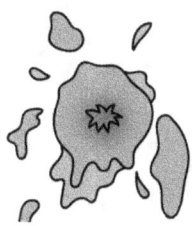

That was all about me. What about YOU?

What are you doing to make your journey of change EASYer on yourself? 🙂 (or not ☹)?

What are you using to escape your situation?

_____

_____

What bad habits are making up for your unmet needs?

_____

_____

_____

_____

Do you think it's possible that life could be better somehow?

_____

Who can you reach out to connect with right now, just to say "Hi!"?

_____

_____

_____

Chapter 3: "NEWer Dave"
Monday, December 11, 2017

The only thing that is constant is change.

Heraclitus

This is a photo of the little coffee shop where I often hang out to write. Hang out, not hide out. Hang out when I am visiting my sweetheart. I sometimes refer to it as my office away from my home office. One of them. I have several writing hang-outs now. I am having a lot of fun writing (and sharing what I write).

Dear Diary: Sutton. Eastern Townships. Just South of Montreal. Monday, December 11, 2017.

I think it's time to move on. I feel sad today. I'm also feeling a little scared. What's with that? It's been almost seven years now since I hit rock bottom, sitting in that food court, isolated, all by myself on that Monday morning. I've worked so hard to get to where I am today. I've changed so much. I feel like I'm a new person. My brother-in-law refers to me as NEW Dave, the change has been that dramatic.

I've changed physically, mentally, emotionally and even spiritually – a word that wasn't part of my vocabulary until a little over a year ago. My change statistics speak for themselves, and I've been keeping track of them (it must be the accountant in me). I'll share them with you in Chapter 4. They tell the story in black and white. I've undergone enough change over the past seven years to last a lifetime. And, unlike the change I went through in the past, this change has been enjoyable and energizing. I am on a roll these days. I am having so much fun. Yes, fun! Apparently, having fun is very important to me. It is part of my newly discovered or re-discovered personality and preferences and communication style, etc. No wonder I was so miserable back in those nasty days. It's hard to have fun and feel the emotions that go with having fun when you tune out your emotions and almost everyone around you. I'll be 53 in a little more than a month and I'm healthier today than in my thirties. My doctor told me recently that I have the heartbeat of a 20-year-old. I eat healthy. I exercise frequently. I get enough sleep. I haven't had an alcohol buzz in nearly two years. The time and energy spent planning for my early retirement have gone into taking a shot at entrepreneurship for the first time in my life. I hope to have a sustainable business by the time I turn 55. Yes, the irony of the change in my definition of my Freedom 55 plan is not lost on me. Quite the change. A new Freedom 55 plan for NEW (or NEWer) Dave.

I'm connecting daily with clients and colleagues and peers around the world. I'm spending quality time with my family and friends. I'm in a loving and caring and very special relationship with a beautiful, loving and caring woman (Qita) who has two beautiful daughters who are also now part of my life. And I can't forget my two beautiful children; they are the loves of my life. I've never felt closer to them. Not only am I spending time with them, but it's quality time. What I've discovered is that less quantity (of booze, that is) results in more quality (of time, that is) with the kids and others (including myself).

All this positive change and, yet, here I am feeling sad and scared. Here I am, in a coffee shop down the street from my sweetheart's house, feeling a bit lost. This is the third time in the past year that I've scheduled time to sit down and write the final chapter of this book. It's time to wrap up this half-time journey of mine and move on to the second half of my life. So, here I am, ready to type up my final few thoughts before heading off for what I thought would be a second-half journey of bliss and a constant state of happiness and fun. Yet, here I am, sad and scared. Am I a fraud? Have I failed in my transition? What gives? Or, in this case, what does not give?

Well, you know what, buddy? Sad and scared are emotions. That sadness you feel is normal. Your kids are with their mother for the rest of the week. You're going to miss them. You love them more than anything. Of course, you're going to feel sad on the Mondays when they're gone. Remember how you feel on the Mondays when you expect them back? What a great reason to look forward to a Monday! Have you forgotten the fun you had last Monday? Making the gingerbread house with your daughter? Your nightly bedtime chat with her? Helping her make "slime" and the mess that goes along with making slime? What about watching the New York Jets' game with your son? There was a lot of yelling and screaming and hooting going on – from both of you. You don't even remember who won. It doesn't matter, it was fun, and you were connected. Oh, and don't forget decorating the Christmas tree and putting up all the lights in the house. That was a lot of fun! Long gone are the days of spending time with the kids accompanied by a bottle or two of wine — one of your crutches to get through life back then.

Back then, but not now, and I am so grateful. Okay, so every once in a while, I'm going to feel sad, but feeling the joy and happiness that come from connecting with my loved ones is what I feel most often — that and the feelings that come from having a lot of fun. The fear you're feeling today is normal, too. After more than 30 years of bi-weekly paycheques, you're now two years from having launched your own business. It's going to take time to get that business going. It's going to take time for the money to start coming in. Not having money coming in regularly is a pretty scary proposition. No wonder your fears pop up every now and then. Remember the book your mom shared with you all those years ago, *Do What You Love, the Money Will Follow*?[3] Well, guess what? You're doing what you love. Can you see the passion in your eyes? Can you hear it in your voice? Can you feel it in your heart?

Yes, I can! Those feelings I shut out and ignored for most of my life are actually proving quite helpful. I also seem to be having a whole lot of fun. Others have also sensed my love and passion and have told me so. How cool is that? How loving and caring is that? And to think that, in the nasty old days, not only was I shutting out my emotions, I was shutting out those others. Shutting out, not just those others, but almost everyone else, including myself.

Well, you've come a long way, baby! You're doing what you love. You're spending time with your loved ones. Quality time with your loved ones. Quality time with your children and family and a very special and beautiful woman. You are connecting and engaging and re-energizing yourself with your colleagues and peers, not just occasionally, but often. You're helping others undertake positive changes in their lives. That's quite a change from seven years ago. You're also spending quality time with yourself. Taking care of yourself. Trusting in yourself. Believing in yourself. Having faith in yourself. Forgiving yourself. Loving yourself.

Yes, that's a lot of progress, buddy. Kudos to you for finally deciding to make that change. Kudos to you for all the progress you've made on this journey of change. Kudos for developing the strength and courage to stay the course, even when things got tough. You'll need that courage for the next leg of your journey.

You see, at least I realize now that life is a journey and not a destination. And, yes, as part of that journey, it's time to finally move on to that second half, messy as it may turn out to be. Your life is not "perfect." It never will be. You are not perfect. You never will be. But that doesn't mean your life isn't great! Screw perfection, you've made a whole lot of progress, you have learned you are a great person, worthy of your kids' love, Qita's love, the love of your family and friends. You don't have to go it alone. You will still have the good, the bad, and the ugly – but now you have a lot more "great."

Now it's time to spend more time helping others with their half-time journeys of change. I am proud of you. I LOVE YOU. I guess I always have. I just forgot it somewhere along the way. Well, I promise not to forget that again and, if I do, please don't hesitate to remind me.

Enjoy your second half with the kids, your sweetheart, your family and, most of all, yourself. There's sure to be more ups and downs moving forward. After all, life is a roller-coaster ride. This time around, though, you're going to have fun riding that roller-coaster because, in the end, it's all over way too soon. So, enjoy the ride, buddy. All of the Mondays and all of the days in between all those Mondays will make up the second half of your life. Bring it on! ☺

SO, WHAT DID I LEARN?

How did I make change EASYer on myself ☺ (or not ☹)?

If life really is a journey and not a destination, and the only constant is change, that means there's a lot more change in my future, regardless of how far I've come – a fact that one of my fellow coaches pointed out to me the other day. She suggested I consider referring to myself as NEWer Dave instead of NEW Dave in order to reflect that constant state of change. Not a bad suggestion. Good thing I discovered that I really enjoy learning and growing and changing. It turns out that Learning and Growth (L&G) represent one of my top values. It is Value #2 on my Top 502 List of Values, right after Family, which is my #1. It took me a while to figure that one out (i.e. Family being #1) because it was not on the previous Top 10 List at all, but that's another story for later.

Good thing I've become more adept at change, and that one of my key enablers of that change is self-love. I mention self-love because, if I had to choose only one thing that allowed me to make and maintain all the change that was part of my half-time transition, it would be my newfound habit of practising self-love. At some point, I had stopped loving and caring for myself. I am not sure when that happened, but I am so pleased I've started that practice up again. I love you, buddy! ☺

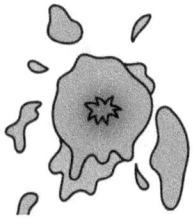

That was all about me. What about YOU?

What are you doing to make your journey of change EASYer on yourself? ☺ (or not ☹)?

How do you react to change? Do you resist, avoid or embrace change?

_____

_____

_____

_____

Where are you on the self-loving spectrum?

_____

_____

Is that okay with you?

_____

_____

What's one nice thing you can do for yourself today that will improve your life or your outlook in some small way?

_____

Chapter 4:
The BEFORE and AFTER Metrics

Transition: A noun of action derived from Latin "transitionem" meaning going across or over.

Here's Old Dave before January 2011 and New Dave after November 2015. They say that a picture is worth a thousand words. If so, what does this one say?

People don't recognize me these days, even people who have known me for years. They have come up to me at events to apologize for not saying hello earlier because they hadn't recognized me. As previously mentioned, my brother-in-law now refers to me as NEW Dave.

I've lost close to one-third of my body mass (er, body fat). Three days before my fiftieth birthday, I weighed in at my normal weight for the first time in more than 15 years of hovering between being overweight and obese. Talk about a cool birthday present to myself! I went from a size Extra-Large to a Medium in the space of a little over a year and a half. For my birthday present that year, I bought myself a whole new wardrobe. Out with the old and in with the new! I live in a city that has four seasons, so it cost me a fortune, but I'm not complaining. I've read that nine out of 10 people who lose weight will gain it back within a year. Some will gain back even more. Yikes! I was highly motivated to not let that happen to me! I don't think I can afford the money or the shopping time!

In fact, I've kept the weight off for more than a couple of years now, so I'm pleased to report that I'm one of the 10% crowd. Good for me, but I can't help feeling badly for the other 90%. I was there before, and I didn't enjoy the experience, or the feelings and the lack of energy that went with it. You see, things had gotten pretty nasty for me around that time. Not only was I out of shape physically, but I eventually got to the point where I had become a clinically depressed, socially-isolated, functioning alcoholic. Quite the mouthful. I was sad. I was lonely. I was scared. I was not in a good place. But, I'm in a good place now and I'm so grateful for the change.

They say a picture is worth a thousand words. If so, take a peek at my "before and after collage" in Chapter 27, the one with the Top 10 change enablers that supported that transition, and you'll get the picture, pardon the pun. Oh, and if you don't think that pictures are the way to tell a story, I invite you to take a look at my "before and after statistics" on the next page. Analytics are all the rage these days. Check mine out!

My before and after stats. What a difference a few years can make...

Category	BEFORE Jan, 2011	AFTER Nov, 2015
Physical ME	• Obese (BMI 33: 264lbs) • Zero exercise, I mean ZERO • On medication for Cholesterol levels, both good and bad levels are off • Pre-diabetic sugar levels • Blood Pressure and heart rate unhealthy	• Healthy weight (BMI 24.4, 190 lbs). New wardrobe. Clothes size M instead of XL. • Exercise 5-6 days a week including cardio & weights • Both cholesterol levels healthy. No longer on MEDS • Sugar levels heathy • Blood pressure and heart rate healthy
Mental ME	• Clinically depressed • Terrified to wander out of my comfort zone • Functioning alcoholic (4-6 bottles of wine per week and/or a dozen beers)	• Waking up in the morning excited for the adventures ahead, even on Mondays • Maximum 1-2 glasses of alcohol (1-2 times per week) • I have not had a buzz from alcohol in over 2 years
Emotional ME	• Avoiding my feelings by not thinking of them • Escaping life by watching movies and reading the newspaper • Emotions? Guys don't talk about Emotions!	• Exploring and acknowledging my feelings and the feelings of others • Sharing and further exploring feelings with others via my Coaching and Storytelling (and my LIFE)
Relationship ME	• Isolated. Shutting out everyone but my 2 children • Connecting with others was never a priority	• Reconnected and close to family and friends • Stronger, quality relationship with my children (now joint custody). • Large network of colleagues and peers (1,000+)
Career ME	• 2009. DP (Developmental Performance): Lowest performance rating in my 13+ years at my former employer • Stuck in MY Comfort Zone • Miserable in my "role" but "paralysed" to do anything about it	• 2013. EP (exceptional performance): Highest performance rating in my 19+ years at my former employer • Directing Global programs at my former employer • Speaking, facilitating and coaching on topics that terrified me only a few years earlier
Romantic ME	• My love language? Say what? • Like the "Grinch Who Stole Christmas", my heart was three sizes too small	• My top 2 LOVE languages are quality time and physical touch • Spending time in MY SOULMATE quadrant is a priority
Spiritual ME	• I did not even know what spiritual meant	• I am uncovering a spiritual side to me that I did not even know existed

As impressive as the positive changes were on the outside, they paled in comparison to the changes that have taken place on the inside. And, I don't mean my internal organs, although some of those had actually shifted location as a result of my extra body fat. By "inside," I'm referring to my mental and emotional state. I'm referring to my heart and my soul. You can't see those changes in a picture. Like *The Grinch who Stole Christmas*, my heart has also grown three sizes but, unlike Mr. Grinch, it took me more than a day.

I still can't believe the change. More like a transformation. I never imagined I'd end up where I am today. My life is no longer the same. Not only have I made and maintained the physical change, I have also made significant changes on the career and relationship sides of my life, on the romantic and non-romantic sides of the equation. So much for social isolation. So much for being stuck in a rut at work. Those nasty things are all in the past. A past that also includes my bout with clinical depression. Good riddance! I'm not sure I'm even the same person today as I was back then. I never set out to make this significant a change. It took on a momentum of its own. I was just trying to make a few changes, so I wouldn't die and leave my beautiful children without a father. That was my motivator. But more on that later.

Actually, when I look back, the focus on my physical health was only possible after I took care of the issues on the mental side (i.e. my clinical depression). Eating healthily and moving more were not the easiest things to motivate myself to do when I felt so depressed. All I wanted to do was shut everything out – every thought and everybody – with the exception of a pint of beer or a glass of wine. I had trouble getting off the couch because I felt so low. I had trouble breathing because I felt so discouraged and so scared. How was I supposed to summon the energy to exercise?

Apparently, it's a package deal – the physical, the mental, the emotional and the spiritual. As I started out on my transformation, I found it hard to have one without the other. I came across a lot of people, who, despite being very healthy and physically fit, were not in a great spot in their lives. There were holes. For some, exercise was an escape from other parts of their lives that weren't going well. Am I ever glad that I finally figured out the package deal! Or, as the accountant in me likes to refer to it, my "wellness portfolio," a balance of the things (as measured on both the inside and outside), that enable me to lead a healthy, joyful and fulfilling life.

It took me close to 50 years to figure that out, but I get it. I am self-aware now. And in coaching, I learned that self-awareness is nine-tenths of the journey. Awareness is the precursor to making a choice. I am reasonably self-aware now, finally, and that's what makes me so confident I'll never go back. Back to that nasty place, that nasty zone, where I used to hide out, alone, all by myself. I much prefer where I am today, surrounded by my family and friends.

Half-Time and My Second Half. Hey! The Goal Posts Keep Moving!

My second half. I came across the concept recently in a book by Bob Buford, *Halftime: Moving from Success to Significance*.[4] I'm a big football fan, so I related to the analogy of two halves and a half-time. I also like the premise that, according to the author, the second half is more fulfilling and joyful than the first. Others have written on this idea as well.

Apparently, this is a time when many of us stop and ask ourselves an important question: Is this really what my life is supposed to be all about? Is this all there is? Often, something seems to be missing.

Some people decide to disregard the feeling that something is missing and continue down the same path; the rationale being, "that's life," or "we can't have it all." Others decide to explore that question further and end up charting a new course in their lives, their rationale being, "life is what I make it," and, "I'd like to make it more meaningful and fulfilling." This desire for change can be brought on by a crisis, or some other moment of self-reflection. Unfortunately, from what I have read, crisis is usually the catalyst. It was in my case.

I had built myself quite the comfort zone during the first half of my life. I might have stayed there forever, except it got so nasty that I felt I had no choice but to get out. To get out and stay out. I thought that my transformation was complete when I stepped on the scale when I turned 50 and my weight was back to normal. I thought I had transformed myself. I was so proud of myself. I was so excited. In hindsight, I see that was just one change of many that would take place during what I refer to now as my half-time, my transition from the first half of my life to the second half. My journey of life-altering self-transformation had not started out as a journey of life-altering self-transformation. One change led to another and, before I knew it, I was going through big shifts. With each shift, the original intended destination and outcome would change. It would change for the better. I kept reaching for, and wanting, more. It was as if I were heading for an end zone where the goal posts kept shifting!

Eventually, I started to wonder when I was going to start living my second half. I'm actually writing this book more than a year later than planned because I thought my transition of self-transformation would be over by now. It turns out I'm still going through the tail-end of that self-transformation as I write this book.

I'm going on seven years of change. That is a lot of change. I recognize now that it's a good thing I decided to make those changes EASYer on myself when I first set out. The EASYer the better, since I discovered that change and comfort zones go together like oil and water. I eventually got to the point where I was enjoying change. My seven-year journey of self-transformation has so far been one of the most fulfilling and fun periods of my life.

My Journey of Change.
Making It EASYer on Myself and Having FUN while at It!
F**k the "No Pain, No Gain" Approach.

Have there been bumps along the road during my journey of self transformation? Yes, and there still are. Have there been difficult periods? Yes, and there still are. Have there been painful moments? Yes, and there still are. But in hindsight, they've been few and far between. And there could have been fewer still, if that's what I had wanted, once I realized that it was all up to me.

When it came to making change, the decisions were all mine to make: I could choose whether or not to make the decisions in the first place, and then I got to choose how to go about making them. I figured that, if every decision were my choice, then it made sense to make them in a way that made things as easy as possible on me. Having fun while I was at it also became part of my modus operandi. I lost close to 100 pounds of body fat and rarely broke a sweat. You will see, as I share my story with you throughout this book, that I tried to make it EASYer on myself and, when I look back on my journey now, that approach served me well. It has been quite the fun journey. And I like to have fun. I'll leave the painful approaches to the "others." I think that those "others" refer to themselves as "suckers for pain." To each his (or her) own.

Oh! And Why Am I Picking on Mondays?

What made me decide to call this book *MONDAYS don't have to SUCK!* Why am I singling out and picking on Mondays? The short answer is because they picked on me. They SUCKED! For a long F**KING time.

I let Mondays do it to me, but that's no excuse. Bad Monday! No wonder no one likes you. You're not nice. I feared Mondays so much I could never fathom liking Mondays. Talk about a lack of willingness to question one's beliefs! Questioning one's beliefs is a key component of making change. My dread of Mondays got so bad at one point that I started drinking as early as Wednesday because I would get anxious and depressed about the looming Monday. I would have started drinking earlier in the week but, as I mentioned previously, my body could not process that much booze. I couldn't drink on Mondays or Tuesdays; ironically, the day I needed my self-prescribed alcoholic medication the most was Monday.

Apparently, I'm not alone in my dislike of Mondays. In my blog "Not Dave's Top 5 List. Top 5 Reasons Why Not EVERYONE Hates Mondays"[5], I have found only two people so far who don't share that feeling of dread for Mondays and I wanted to join them. In my case, I didn't want to just like Mondays, but to love them—and all the rest of the days of the week, as well. Well, I am getting close to that goal. Getting close to enabling that transition, that shift, that mind and heart shift, and once I am there, it will be time to maintain it. And what better way to maintain it than to make it a habit? How cool a habit would that be? To get up every day of the week, Mondays included, and look forward to that day, looking forward to having an awesome day. Here's to making that one a habit! Monday, I'm sorry for all the terrible things I've said about you. I'm looking forward to the start of a great relationship!

SO, WHAT DID I LEARN?

How did I make change EASYer on myself ☺ (or not ☹)?

Who knows? Maybe now that I have started making all of these changes and have come to realize how positive an impact they can have on me and my loved ones, I might just keep moving the goal posts out further and further. Maybe my half-time will end up a little longer than first planned. Maybe a lot longer. Until death do us part. The more often that I move the goal posts, the more I grow. The more I grow, the more connected I feel with myself and others. There are speed bumps along the way, as the rest of me and my foundation catch up, but does it ever feel great when they do. ☺

Oh! And, by the way, although it was not my intention at the time, my new healthier ways are having a secondary positive effect. A bit of a bonus: they are rubbing off on my children. While grocery shopping with me the other day, my son pointed out to me, after reading the ingredients on a container of food, that there was too much salt. "Put it back on the shelf, Dad," he said. Wow! I'm setting the example of leading a healthy lifestyle for my children. Hopefully that will make it EASYer on them later in their lives. ☺

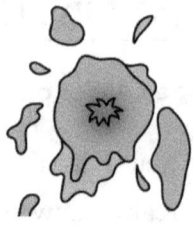

That was all about me. What about YOU?

What are you doing to make your journey of change EASYer on yourself? ☺ (or not ☹)?

What do you dread?

_____

_____

_____

What is stopping you from doing something about it?

_____

_____

_____

What's one thing you can do right now to bring yourself closer to ending that feeling of dread?

_____

_____

_____

> **OLD DAVE**
> **1965 - TBD**
>
> He lived his life in his comfort zone.
>
> May he rest in peace.

Chapter 5:
My Imperative for Changing My Epitaph

In any given moment, we have two options. To step forward into growth, or to step back into safety.

Abraham Maslow

Here lies David Arthur Walker. He lived his life in his comfort zone. NOT! Almost. But NOT!

I'm a big movie fan. I have more than 1,000 DVDs. One of my favourite movie scenes is in the movie *Braveheart*, when William Wallace shouts his motivational message to the troops, "Everybody dies, but not everyone truly lives!" As it turns out, I was not truly living my life. Not during the first half of my life anyway. I wasn't aware of that at the time. I am now.

March 2017. Reflecting Back on OLD Dave, Captain Comfort Zone. And His Old Epitaph.

Was it a terrible life? No, at least not in the beginning. With a few exceptions, it was pretty good. I had the career, and the wife, and the kids, and the colleagues, and the caring family, and the house, and the retirement funds, and all that stuff. I was sitting pretty. I was in a pretty comfortable place. I had spent a lot of time building myself a comfortable space. A pretty comfortable zone, MY COMFORT ZONE.

But one day, MY COMFORT ZONE turned into MY NASTY ZONE. As I tried to make my way out, I realized it was built very solidly. I also realized that, while I was in there, I had started to give up on life. I had started to settle for less. I had stopped growing. I had stopped connecting. I had stopped living. I had stopped loving. My love bucket[6] was pretty much running on empty. I had stopped loving everyone but my children. I had stopped loving everyone, including myself. I had shut them all out. And, as you will read, and see in the photographs in this book, that didn't serve me well at all.

I had given up on truly living my life in return for living a life of comfort. I had given up on my hopes and dreams. I had landed solidly in my comfort zone (my settling-for-less-in-life zone). Then, when it turned nasty and I started to try to crawl my way out, I soon realized I was trapped. And by "soon," I mean it took me more than 40 years to come to that realization. Wow! I'm kind of thankful for the onset of that nasty period in my life. It was a wake-up call. A mid-life wake-up call. Now I know where the term "mid-life crisis" comes from. My life was ticking away. So was my physical and mental health. And, as with everything in life, I had a choice. MY choice was to either listen to (what

I now realize) was a wake-up call and try to do something about it, or to ignore that call and hope that things would get better on their own.

I decided to make a change, rather than wait for one. Not a transformation. Just a change. All I could think of at the time was the next step. Not steps, I couldn't think that far ahead. All I could come up with was just One Next Step. My next step was the decision to quit my job. I had nothing lined up at the time. I had been with the same employer for almost 15 years. I was part of the furniture. And, although I didn't know it at the time, I was clinically depressed. I had slowly become an obese, socially-isolated, functioning alcoholic suffering from a serious mental health challenge. That was sometime in March 2010. And I just did it. I went into my boss' office to quit. I didn't tell my wife. I didn't tell anyone. That was almost exactly seven years ago. As it turns out, it was one of the lowest points in my life. I've since made an agreement with myself to never let that happen again.

Things didn't turn out the way I thought they would that day back in March 2010 in my now ex-boss' office, but more on that later. As fate would have it, things haven't turned out the way I thought they would on many occasions during these years of change. I had no idea that I was about to embark upon a seven-year-plus journey. I had no idea that I would end up where I am now. Transforming was not my intention at the time. At the time, all I wanted to do was to end the pain and suffering. And I did.

Not only did I end the pain and suffering, but I replaced them with what I can only describe as the polar opposite: living a life of meaning and personal and professional fulfilment and fun. It took a lot of work. It took a lot of courage. In my case, at my pace, it took a lot of time. But

I did it. I pulled it off. I changed my epitaph from, "He lived his life in his comfort zone," to "He did his best to live every day to the fullest."

Who knows, maybe I will change it again. The more I change, the more I want to change. My life just seems to keep getting better and better these days. My life with me. My life with my friends and my loved ones. And that's a good thing for me, and my friends and my loved ones, because life is short, and time passes by, oh, so fast. The one thing we can't change in life is that, like it or not, we will eventually die. That's when our final epitaph will be written. We can't change our epitaph after we die. It's too late. But we can change it before then. We don't have to change it. It's our choice. If you like yours, great. Don't change it. I didn't like mine, so I chose to change it. Am I ever glad I did, and I hope the choices I made might inspire you to write a few new chapters in yours!

My Superhero Transition: Playing to My Super Powers From "Captain Comfort Zone to "CAPTAIN COURAGEOUS"

Okay, so I'm over 50 and still believe in superheroes. Sue me. I like superheroes. I think that deep down everyone is born super. Everyone is born with superhero strengths. It just takes time to find our super powers. It takes time for a number of reasons. Often, it's because others keep telling us which ones we should choose. Which ones we should develop. People mean well, but often their advice is based on themselves and their lens and not on those of the unique super person they're trying to help. Oh, and guess what? Your superhero powers can change over time. Who knew? I'm grateful for that. Really grateful. Do you know why? Because I realized I was "Captain Comfort Zone" and that was not serving me well.

My super power was building comfort zones. Building and maintaining them. And I was really good at building my Comfort Zone and staying in it. And keeping others out. I had developed strategies and frameworks and tool kits. I had physically built multiple comfort zones, including a multi-year project to build a Comfort Home. And to top it off, I developed a Comfort Dream. A dream to end all dreams: I was going to retire at 55 and have all the money I would ever need and all the time in the world to enjoy it. My strategy, in this case, was currently being enabled by my Freedom 55 plan which entailed basically giving up on life for 10 years while I saved enough money to enjoy it later. If I lasted that long.

Luckily for me, a new superhero was going to appear on the scene and rescue me. Rescue me from me. It was going to be none other than ME. Yes, ME! A new ME – Captain Courageous! It took a while to realize he had shown up and wanted to help but realize it I did, finally. He was there. He had my back. And not only did he care for me, he loved me. When I realized how loving and caring he was toward me, we really started to work together. And you know what happened when that little piece of self-awareness hit home? Captain Comfort Zone didn't stand a chance. Despite the years he had spent building my Comfort Zones and making them strong, he didn't stand a chance when I, with the help of Captain Courageous, started to develop my self-confidence. It wasn't even a fair fight. Captain Comfort Zone got one hell of an ass-kicking. I'm hoping we don't see much more of him. Good riddance!

You see, the bottom line is that my story of self-transformation is a story of courage. How I summoned the courage to make a very significant life change. How I developed the courage to not only overcome a very dark period in my life, but to keep moving forward and changing until I came to a really awesome place. This level of courage has helped me to stay the course, even when nasty Captain Comfort Zone comes back, every now and then. I was hoping he would go away forever, but I realize that he's still hanging around, waiting for an opportunity to come back and play. Unlike in the past, I am aware of his presence and the nasty things that happen when I listen to him. So, here's hoping and, more importantly, believing, I don't let him.

SO, WHAT DID I LEARN?

How did I make change EASYer on myself ☺ (or not ☹)?

Choice. In the end, we all have a choice. It certainly does not feel that way at times, but the more I think of it, and the more I try it out, the more I believe it to be true. But, as they like to tell us in coaching, in order to make a change, you have to believe in yourself and in your change. That might mean challenging some long-held perceptions and beliefs but, if you don't believe that you have a choice and/or a chance, it is pretty hard to even get started. And not getting started is no way to make change EASYer on yourself. ☹ Oh, and a little courage also comes in handy, after all, it can get scary along the way.

And speaking of "along the way…" What does that really mean? Someone shared a poem with me recently. It is called "*The Dash*" by Linda Ellis[7]. The dash is referenced as the time between our birth and our death. In the poem, a man is speaking at the funeral of a friend. (See the endnote for the website URL where you can access the whole poem.) It is worth a peek in its entirety, but I wanted to share three excerpts with you:

He noted that first came the date of her birth

And spoke of the following date with tears

But he said what mattered most of all

Was the dash between those years

......

So, think about this long and hard;

Are there things you'd like to change?

For you never know how much time is left

That can still be rearranged

.....

So, when your eulogy is being read

With your life's actions to rehash

Would you be proud of the things they say

About how you spent your dash?

So, Mister Walker. What is your choice? Enjoy your dash or coast to the finish line of life? Remember, it is your choice!

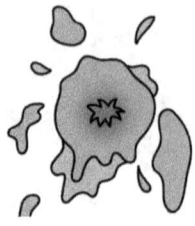

That was all about me. What about YOU?

What are you doing to make your journey of change EASYer on yourself? ☺ (or not ☹)?

Are you enjoying your Dash more often than not?

_____
_____
_____

Are you dashing with the people you want to be dashing with?

_____
_____
_____

What is going to happen if you don't change the path you're on?

_____
_____
_____

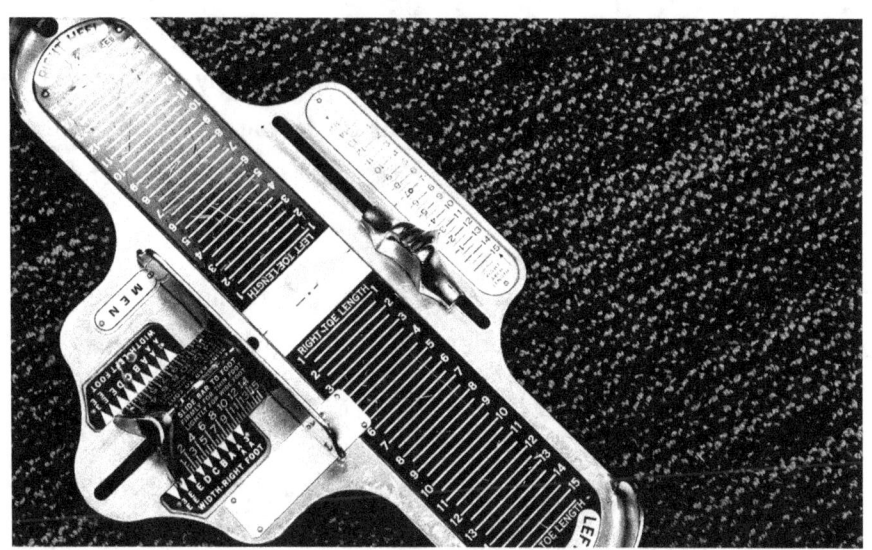

Chapter 6: Contemplating a Change to Your Epitaph?

Life is a daring adventure or nothing at all.
Helen Keller

I took a picture of this handy little tool when buying shoes recently. Recognize it? What better analogy for change than trying on a new pair of shoes! It's all about trying something out in order to find the best fit. You can measure it first, but you're only really sure that the shoe fits after you've tried it on and tried it out.

Sharing My Story in the Hopes of Inspiring and/or Empowering Yours.

In his book *Halftime*, Bob Buford describes the purpose of half-time as a time "to take stock, to listen, and to learn."[8] Well, I took stock and I listened. I finally listened to myself and to others and, most importantly, to my heart. And I learned. I learned a lot and I would like to share some of those insights and lessons learned in this book. For those of you who would like more details on any of the specific topics or concepts that I explore in this book, you may find some of my blogs of interest. They're archived on my website.[9] I'll reference them wherever relevant. What can I say, I like to share!

I realize that everyone is unique. Everyone has unique dreams and aspirations, and a unique situation that is changing all the time. Will what I'm sharing work for you? Some of the things I tried as part of my journey worked for me, and some did not. It was only by trying them that I was able to identify which ones worked for me and which did not. My hypothesis is that you will find what does and does not work for you in the same way, by trying them out. I love the saying "we don't know what we don't know." If you think about it, everything is theory until we make it real. So, go ahead and try some of the ideas I'm sharing with you and, once you do, don't be shy about reaching out and sharing some back. After all, I didn't come up with anything new, I just tried a bunch of stuff and stuck with what worked for me. I found my fit, like a pair of properly-fitting shoes and, before I knew it, I was off to the races.

Beg, Borrow and Steal. Find Your Fit. Go for It.

This is my journey. My experience. My story. If you can glean something from it, use it. I didn't come up with anything new. Why reinvent the wheel when there is so much already out there? As a very wise man once told me, "Beg, borrow and steal." Everything here is yours for the taking. So, beg, borrow and steal away. I insist. You don't even have to beg. Steal away! You won't go to jail. Leverage what works for you and, by you, I mean the Unique You.

As part of my coaching training, I was spending a lot of time on myself and my personal foundation. I decided to take a year off to explore the topic. Instead of backpacking around the world during my sabbatical or searching for meaning on remote mountain tops, I decided to learn all about myself and the process of self-transformation. Over the course of my journey thus far, I have read more than 100 self-help books. I've taken dozens of self-assessments and I've read and watched as much as I could on the topic of self-discovery and self-transformation. I've also connected with more than 200 people to exchange notes and takeaways on the subject. I found that most of what I had read, and most of what people had told me, was really just about theories that had been filtered through the lenses of other people's personal lives. It was about what had worked for them in their own situations.

I decided the best approach was to make the theories real for me. That's when the magic happened. That's when the learning and growing really started. That's when I started having "Ah-ha" moments – when stuff started to stick. Trying things out and, just as importantly, processing each experience (i.e. taking time to reflect on what I had done and what I had learned from it). As I now like to tell people, "I believe a quarter of what I hear, half of what I see, but 100% of what I do."

As you read my book, you'll see I tried a lot of stuff. I made a lot of theory real. It was not always easy. It often took courage, and I was more into being comfortable in those days. But I tried them out and, what didn't kill me made me all the more courageous; hopefully, there will be something in my story that inspires you to take action.

Are You Ready to Go? Are You Ready to Make It Real? If I can inspire you to explore or rewrite your epitaph, nothing would please me more. If reading my story brings out more courage in you, nothing would make me happier.

SO, WHAT DID I LEARN?

How did I make change EASYer on myself ☺ (or not ☹)?

Make the theory real. Just do it. Just try it out, or try it on for size and fit. There is no "one size fits all" in the pursuit of self-awareness and self-transformation. In his book, *The Four Agreements*[10], author Don Miguel Ruiz challenges us to do away with assumptions and focus on creating Hypotheses. Unlike our assumptions, which the author reminds us are most often wrong, hypotheses can be tested in order to determine what is real, and what is not. Testing things in order to make them real, not assuming something that, more often than not, turns out to be wrong. I can't think of an EASYer way to explore change. ☺

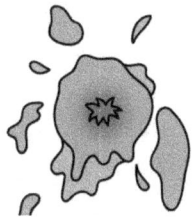

That was all about me. What about YOU?
What are you doing to make your journey of change EASYer on yourself? ☺ (or not ☹)?

When they finalize the details on your epitaph, what do you want it to read?

_____

_____

What forms of significance can you start inserting in the success part of your life goals?

_____

_____

How will you know what is significant to you?

_____

_____

Short of a sabbatical, how can you make the time and reduce the stress involved in enabling your change?

_____

A comfort zone is a beautiful place but nothing grows there.
Unknown

PART 2
My First Half: Captain Comfort Zone (1965-2008)

Chapter 7: My Search for Success

Try not to become a man of success.
Rather become a man of value.

Albert Einstein

Of all the photographs of my youth, this one of me on vacation in Myrtle Beach sums it up best. A care-free, cozy and comfortable life growing up. That's me on the diving board – well before I hit 264 lbs on the scale! ☹

January 22, 1965 to July 1983. My "Formative" Years.

The early years. What some people refer to as our "formative years." For me, this was a happy time. A healthy time. When I look at photo albums from those days, I'm amazed at how fit and happy I looked growing up. I remember a loving and caring family, family trips, friends in the neighbourhood and at school, my best friend and next-door neighbour, playing lots of sports. I don't remember being much of a scholar (especially in math), but I got by. I basically grew up in a very comfortable place. A very comfortable zone that was free of abuse, bullying, divorce, wars, poverty, unemployment, mental illness, alcoholism, or drugs. None of those existed in my zone. I played with friends in the summer, made a bit of money from a summer job, went to school, and, when I graduated from school, I planned to get a job, get married, buy a house, pursue my career, save for retirement and eventually retire. I wanted to retire early, ideally, so that my wife and I could live happily ever after, touring the world and living a life of bliss as the sun slowly set on what was, for all intents and purposes, a successful life. That was my lens growing up. That's how I saw the world. It shaped my definition of success: the career, the love of my life, the kids, the car, the house, the white picket fence. Ah! The sweet smell of success! As I was packing to head off to university, it was all in my sights and in my dreams. Dream life, here I come!

August 1983 – May 1994. The "Trying to Find Myself" Years. Alone.

They say that most people don't know what they want to do when they head off to university. Count me in that group! But off to university I went. Heaven forbid I didn't go to university! That was, after all, the next step on the journey to success. But what should I study? Forget science or arts or engineering. Let's see now? How about business? A business degree sounds interesting. I'll get one of those. It was my first time away from home so, although I quickly discovered that business school was not all it was cracked up to be, for me, anyway, I was having enough fun on the extra-curricular front to tough it out on the academic front. But there was only so much partying that my summer-job savings could fund, so my first experience in university ended prematurely, after two years, with no degree in sight. I would go back to school eventually and finish my undergraduate degree on a part-time basis. A very part-time basis. The other part of that time was spent trying to figure out what I wanted to do in this great big world of business. Over the following eight years I changed jobs and careers more often than my underwear and didn't make a whole lot of cash doing it.

At first, I thought I was going to have a career in hospitality, then in retail, then in banking, then in accounting, then in financial analysis, then in investment management, the list goes on. Meanwhile, my friends were starting to execute on their roadmap to success. They had jobs, got married, had kids, saved money, bought houses and cottages. I was still working part-time on my degree, moving from job to job, with no savings to speak of and, for most of that time, living alone, spending a lot of time alone, with no girlfriend. Yes, I had been single for the first 30+ years of my life, mostly. I was fast approaching the big 3-0 and the longest relationship I had had with a woman had lasted less than two months.

Good thing that I got along well with myself in those days. I was spending most of my time alone. So much for finding the love of my life. I had to spend time with women for that to happen. So much for the dream house. Houses cost money and, as I approached my thirtieth birthday, I had none. I had recently been fired from my job, so no job and, to top it all off, very little money in the bank – and no assets. Well, no assets, except for my university degree, which I had finally managed to complete after six years. Oh, I did have one other asset at the time. I didn't realize it then, but it was worth a lot. A whole lot! And it was going to be worth even more in the future.

That asset was ME. If, you don't believe me, take a look at my blog on "Have You Updated Your Balance Sheet Lately?"[11] Although I took a lot of accounting courses over the years, none of them emphasized what I personally consider to be the most valuable asset of them all, ME! Or, in your case, YOU!

So, although I thought I had neither accomplished nor amounted to much during that period, especially when I compared myself to others, I had myself, my family and my friends and, as you will read later in my story, that was plenty. More than plenty.

September 1994 – April 1996. Back to School. For Real, This Time.

In the spring of 1994, the money that was funding the "trying to find myself" phase of my life had pretty much dried up and I was sleeping on the floor of a friend's house on an inflatable bed that kept losing air. Not the most uplifting of environments. I don't remember seeing that phase in any journey-to-success book. It was depressing. It was scary. I felt destitute. I can still remember phoning my mom and telling her how discouraged I felt. I am so grateful to have had someone in my life I could reach out to and connect with. I was lonely and frightened. It was time to regroup. It was time to move back home. Just so you know, the house milestone on my journey-to-success checklist meant buying and living in my own home, not moving back to live in my parents' home.

Oh, and good luck finding the love of your life now. I was almost 30 years old and living in my old bedroom with no job and no savings. That sure wasn't going to attract a whole lot of single women. What now? My self-esteem was so low that I couldn't think of looking for another job. I had zero energy and even less self-confidence. Why bother sending out résumés? No one is going to give me the time of day, much less spend the time in an interview. I was sleeping on someone's floor not that long ago, for Pete's sake. So, let's see now. What do I do? How about going back to school? If at first you don't succeed, then perhaps another degree will do the trick. MBA, here I come! And, just to be on the safe side, I'll get my accounting designation at the same time. If three times is the charm, then three degrees/designations should make me more charming.

May 1996. My Career Has Come a'Calling. Time to Join the Real World. The Corporate World. Fasten Your Seat Belt!

I enjoyed university a lot more the second time around. I graduated with my MBA on the dean's honour list. I was also among the top 10 graduates in my province on the accounting designation front. It's incredible what you can do when you put your mind to it. Your mind, and your time. I had lots of time because I had spent the whole two years as a bachelor and had no relationships with women whatsoever. At least I was enjoying the learning this time. And guess what? By the time I finished my studies, I had a job offer. Actually, I had a couple of job offers. Those offers led to a job, which in turn led to a promotion, which in turn led to meeting my future wife, which in turn led to marrying my wife, which in turn led to buying a house, and so on, and so on. Yes, I had finally embarked upon my journey to success. As the managing partner at the firm that hired me told me at the time, at age 31 I was a little late to the game, but better late, than never.

And once I arrived, I caught up fast. Both my wife and I had well-paying jobs and, as the years went by, promotions and raises, and the accumulation of assets, rolled in. The home was purchased and paid for within seven years; two debt-free cars were parked in the driveway within four years; and the retirement nest egg was starting to grow and grow. Before I knew it, we were in the top tier of the wealthiest people in the country. Not bad, if I do say so myself, and all that took place in less time than it took me to finish my undergraduate degree. Mind you, I was traveling all the time for work, but that still left weekends to catch up with my wife. I was starting to make real progress on the career front. I was becoming a veteran. I was becoming a specialist. For the first time in my life, I was really starting to find my way around and I was becoming good at something. Something I enjoyed that I felt could last.

Before I knew it, I was becoming part of the fabric at work. I was feeling pretty comfortable. I was feeling successful. I was feeling safe. I didn't know it at the time, but I was starting to live in my comfort zone, not to mention, starting to do some serious planning for my retirement comfort zone. How comforting is that? My discovering-myself days were now a thing of the past. I wasn't going back there again, not when my present was so successful and, not to mention, comfortable.

April 2004. It's a Boy. Welcome to Parenthood, Mr. Walker!

Career? Check! Wife? Check! House? Check! Two cars? Check! Savings? Check! Dog? No, but we have a cat, so check! Kids? Check! Two beautiful children. One of each. The first arrived in April 2004; the second, shortly thereafter, in June 2006. Kids, the latest addition, but certainly not the least, on the checklist of life success. They were not only another checkmark for my successful life but also another ball to juggle in the balancing act in my life of work, rest and play.

It was also time to cut back on the travel. I had been traveling extensively as part of my new career. What we called the 3-4-5 model: three nights in a hotel, four days at the client site and the fifth day was spent working at home or in the office on behalf of the client. I couldn't possibly travel as much and spend time with my kids. My weekends were going to need a little reengineering as well. Weekends with my wife would soon become weekend nights with my wife, and they started at 8:00 p.m. when the kids were in bed and we were both exhausted from our day. How romantic. Oh, well, hang in there, I thought. Freedom 55 is not that far away, and we'll have all the time in the world to spend together then. In the meantime, we can schedule a date night or two.

Oh, and on the travel-less front, I might have to explore new work options in order to make that one work. And by exploring new work options, I mean make changes. It was hard to be successful in my existing role unless I was willing to travel, so a change was probably going to have to be in order…but it had been a while since I had made changes on the workplace front. That sounded really scary! Things were pretty comfy at the time. "It's taken me a while to get to where I am," I thought. "I have become successful. I'm not sure I want to rock the boat. That doesn't sound like something that will make me feel all that comfortable. What if I just sit tight? Freedom 55 isn't that far off. I only have 16 more years to go."

SO, WHAT DID I LEARN?

How did I make change EASYer on myself ☺ (or not ☹)?

Have you heard the expression that "self-awareness is the precursor to self-change?" I was so caught up in a bunch of expectations and preconceived notions of what success was all about that I had pretty much stopped asking myself if I was really enjoying what I was doing and where I was going. "Keeping up with the Joneses" was my strategy for success during the first half of my life. This approach was very much in line with what Bob Buford describes in *HalfTime* as the success-focused first half of one's life. The significance-focused second half would have to wait.

I now believe that I was also really scared at the time, but I was not aware of that feeling, that primal feeling of FEAR, because I was doing everything I could to not feel fear and pain and the result was no longer feeling much at all. ☹

"Just keep moving forward," I would tell myself. "Keep building that comfort zone and comfort home and retirement plan." "Don't rock the boat." I thought I was making things EASYer on myself by keeping my head down and plowing forward and ignoring and avoiding anything and everything that did not feel comfortable. Now that I'm more self-aware (and wiser, hopefully), I realize that I was not. ☹

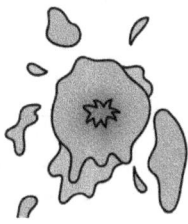

That was all about me. What about YOU?

What are you doing to make your journey of change EASYer on yourself? ☺ (or not ☹)?

What is your definition of success?

_____

_____

Are you checking all the boxes?

_____

Is that actually making you happy?

_____

Is there anything you need to courageously face up to right now about the life you're leading?

_____

_____

Is it possible that something you're afraid of might not be as bad as you think it is?

_____

> The optimist sees opportunity in every Danger. The pessimist sees danger in every opportunity.
> — WINSTON CHurchill

Chapter 8:
The Making of Captain Comfort Zone

Too many of us are not living our dreams because we are living our fears.

Les Brown

I sometimes think that Winston Churchill had me in mind when he wrote his now-famous quote about optimism and opportunity. I was in a place where I saw danger (and failure) lurking in every corner.

Captain Comfort Zone and His Supporting Cast

It had taken me a while to finally start living my life of "success." More than 40 years, to be more precise. I had the wife, the career, the house, the two cars, the kids and the cash to fund that dream retirement. I was living the dream. It seemed like many of my friends were getting divorced, but not me. It seemed like many of my friends were having issues and challenges in various parts of their lives, but not me. Or, so it seemed. I wasn't aware of much at the time, and I wasn't looking too closely at my life. I would have had to look in order to see.

Now I realize that trying not to be aware of things was part of who I was. It was part of who I had become. I avoided anything that might cause me discomfort. Engaging in potential confrontations? Avoid at all costs! Providing feedback that might hurt someone's feelings? Avoid at all costs! Taking action that might lead to failure? Avoid at all costs! Thinking thoughts that might make me feel sad? Avoid at all costs! Yes, somehow during my first half, I had become someone I wouldn't have recognized if I had bothered to look. I had become Captain Comfort Zone. And I had ended up building one hell of a comfort zone! If universities had handed out degrees in building and maintaining comfort zones, I have no doubt I would've been on the Dean's Honour List.

So, without further ado, allow me to introduce David Arthur Walker, also known as Captain Comfort Zone. Yes, there he is! In all his splendour! The shaping of his "formative years" is complete; the influence of his years of "trying to find himself" years is complete. And last, but not least, he has crossed "climb the corporate ladder" and "accumulate wealth" off his bucket list.

Yes, Captain Comfort Zone. Quite the guy! Sadly, as I would find out later – the hard way – that wasn't actually who I really was. It didn't reflect my true personality. But that story is for later. For now, let's get to know Captain Comfort Zone a little better. He's a man of many talents. A man of many faces. Here are but a few masks he's managed to hide behind over the years.

OSTRICH Guy
a.k.a. "Avoider" of Emotions, a.k.a. Non-Emotion guy

My thinking in the old days – the OLD Dave days – was that, if I didn't have to acknowledge negative feelings, then I wouldn't have to deal with any. I applied the same logic to tough discussions. I figured that all the tough stuff would go away, or leave me alone at least, if I ignored it. I thought wrong. It got worse. Like interest on an unpaid loan, the negative feelings just compounded. And if that weren't bad enough, by keeping my head buried in the sand, I didn't experience many positive emotions either. I wasn't connecting and experiencing much of anything.

CAVEMAN Guy
a.k.a. How-to-Avoid-Connecting-with-Other-Humans Guy

If you're not into connecting with people, what better enabler than hanging out in a cave? In my case, I hung out in my "man cave." Now, don't get me wrong, there's nothing wrong with a man spending quality time in his cave. My problem was that I was spending almost all my time in mine. I started to develop my flair for designing and building man caves at a young age. I set up a pretty cool lair in my parents' home that included a waterbed, a TV, a stereo, and a VCR. I set up an equally cozy space in my first apartment. But nothing compares to the cave I built in my house. It included a wine fridge, a beer fridge, a 130-inch movie screen and projector, plus a popcorn machine, a surround-sound system, and more than 1,000 movies in my DVD collection. And, for the odd occasion when I had to venture out of my man cave, I set up "mini-escape pods," household projects like planting trees, mowing the lawn, painting a room, cleaning the car, and so on. I could, and would, spend hours on these projects. I was always alone or with my son. I usually had a beer or two, or three, or more, in hand.

SHY Guy
a.k.a. Liquid-Courage-Needed-at-Social-Gatherings Guy

What I remember about myself when I look back on my formative years is that I was very shy. Shy with people I did not know; especially people in authority like adults and teachers when I was younger, and executives and senior leaders when I was older. I was okay once I got to know people but, until then, connecting with acquaintances and strangers did not come easily. I was not comfortable unless I had a little liquid courage to back me up and, by liquid courage, I mean booze. I discovered at an early age that liquid courage allowed me to open up and be myself. I'm actually a pretty fun and funny guy, if you can get me to relax and come out of my shell. Networking? Hitting the cocktail circuit? Bring it on! As long as there are plenty of cocktails.

CHECKLIST Guy
a.k.a. Lack-of-Self-Awareness Poster Boy. Heads Down. Blinders On.

I have already mentioned the role that checklists played in shaping the latter part of my first half. Career? Check! House? Check! Wife? Check! Kids? Check! COMFORT ZONE? Double Check! Captain Comfort Zone? Triple Check! I was so good at moving through my checklists that I got to a point where I was essentially sleep-walking through life. I was so good at it that, if I had looked up "checklist guy" in the dictionary, I'm sure my photo would have been included with the definition. At least I'm not alone in that. From what I've read and observed, I'm not the only one who has come to the realization that I had been following a checklist. Fortunately, I had the wherewithal to try to deal with it, even if it was a little late in the game. Many people never get that far.

BI-WEEKLY PAYCHEQUE Guy
a.k.a. Risk-Averse Guy

Risk? Did someone mention the word "risk"? Someone close to me once told me that she could never see me as an entrepreneur. She couldn't see me in a situation where I didn't have a regular paycheque coming in. I was just way too risk-averse. I didn't debate her on that, despite having been assessed as having the debater-type personality through a Myers-Briggs self-assessment. At the time, I totally agreed with her. The mere thought of such a situation was enough to make me cringe. There was NO WAY I would ever consider giving up that paycheque. Look up "risk-averse" in the dictionary and you'll possibly see a picture of me there, too.

TECHNICAL Guy
a.k.a. Narrow-Your-Career-Possibilities Guy

If you like comfort zones, especially career-related ones, I highly recommend specializing in just one or two areas, the more technical the better. I did it. I didn't do it intentionally. I enjoyed what I was doing. What was my area of expertise? Nothing exciting. An accounting methodology. I just happened to be among the few who had experience with it. People were reaching out to engage me on the topic. It made me feel confident. It provided a sense of accomplishment. It was my ticket to stardom, my passport for travelling the world. One thing led to another over time, and my area of expertise and my area of comfort became highly specialized – and very narrow, very fast. When I eventually hit the wall – the wall of my comfort zone, that is – I didn't see it coming. I only knew I had to broaden my area of knowledge and capability and opportunities for the sake of my mental and physical health. I couldn't see that my passport to stardom and my ticket to see the world had become an albatross around my neck, weighing me down, keeping me solidly in place. I couldn't see a way out. But I had to get out.

NON-SALES Guy
a.k.a. Hide-under-My-Desk-at-the-Mere-Mention-of-the-S-Word Guy

Can you say "salesperson"? Now, try saying NON-salesperson. That was ME. There was no other word in the English language that had the power to terrify me more than "sales." I have always feared sales. On a few occasions, I forgot my fears. In grade school, I asked for 20 chocolate bars to sell for a fundraiser. I sold one. To my dad. He felt badly for me.

During my "finding myself phase," I actually took on a sales role. It was supposed to be a temporary stepping stone to another opportunity. Well, it was temporary all right; I left that job within the first six months, slinking away like a dog with its tail between its legs. Luckily for me, I had no kids or mortgage at the time. What was I thinking back then? So much for stepping out of my comfort zone. Even in later roles, I knew as I progressed in my career that sales would take on a more important role. I guess I just figured I would cross that bridge when I got to it. Once again, that approach did not work out well. I got stuck. Stuck and depressed and isolated.

YES-MAN Guy
a.k.a. Zero-Boundaries Guy

Just say YES. I don't think I could sum up my modus operandi on the communications front any simpler than that. I used it at work, rest and play. "Dad, can I stay up past bed time?" Yes! "Dave, can you take on another project?" Yes. "Dave, would you like to be part of the new committee?" Yes! "Dave, do you have any boundaries? No!" Aha. Gotcha! Trick question!

Want to bite off more than you can chew? Want to spoil your kids? Want to become emotionally overwhelmed at times? Just say "Yes!" Not just often, not just most of the time, but almost always.

NON-CONFLICT Guy
a.k.a. Ignore-'em-and-They'll-Go-Away Guy

It only seemed logical to me back in the day that, if I wanted to avoid conflict, then I should avoid it. Avoid it at all costs. I didn't like confrontation then (I still don't). In my MBA days, I remember one reading assignment on having tough discussions. I almost wish now I had read it all those years ago when it was first assigned. I wasn't into all that self-help-people-hugging crap back then. I am surprised I kept it, in fact. Captain Comfort Zone certainly had no use for it. But, you know what? Captain Courageous just might. My personal hypothesis is that it takes a lot of courage, on the part of both participants, to engage in a difficult discussion. After all, it takes "two to tango." Hmmm. It might just be time to dust that paper off and learn something new from it.

MR. NICE Guy
a.k.a. Don't-Worry-Be-Happy Guy

Mr. Nice Guy. I have friends who tell me that I'm the nicest person they know. I'm flattered. I believe that this feedback was shared in a positive context. Unfortunately, my motivation in the past for being nice hindered me on the caring side of things. I wasn't big on hurting feelings, so I pretty much let everything go. If someone wanted honest feedback, I was probably not the best person to ask. It's fairly easy to say nice things about people, quite another when there is some strong messaging and/or feedback to share. Sharing it because you want to help the other person. Sharing it because you care about the other person and you want to help them. It takes courage. And in the old days, OLD Dave's courage tank was running on fumes.

SCAREDY CAT
a.k.a. Avoid-All-Things-New Guy

I can't think of a better enabler to force someone into their comfort zone than fear. Somewhere along the way, I had become afraid of a lot of things. I was afraid of trying new things. I was afraid of failing. I was afraid of meeting new people. I got to the point where I dreaded and feared almost any type of change. I tried to hide from change, but it always seemed to catch up with me. It's said that the only constant in life is change. In those days, I had another constant going on and it was related to change. That constant was a fear of change.

Summing It All up

What a mess. Captain Comfort Zone certainly had a nasty cast of characters supporting him. Some are part of his personality and were shaped long ago but a lot, I was to find out, were part of his mindset and had been shaped over a much longer period. And when I say mindset, the growth-oriented kind is not what springs to mind. It was time to work on shifting my mindset. A lot. "Hey, Captain Comfort Zone! Are you sure you're up to the challenge?"

SO, WHAT DID I LEARN?

How did I make change EASYer on myself ☺ (or not ☹)?

Ever hear of the term "emotional intelligence"? You're not born with it; you learn it. When it comes to emotions and emotional intelligence, I had a lot of learning to do and ignoring my emotions was not making it any EASYer on myself. ☹ But, if avoiding my emotions was not serving me well during this period of my life, I was not alone. As authors Dan Kindlon and Michael Thompson point out in their book, *Raising Cain: Protecting the Emotional Life of Boys*[12], there are a lot of other dudes who, at some point, have not been comfortable dealing with their emotions, a whole lot of them.

We "men" (or, "Martians," as John Gray styled us in his popular book on gender differences, *Men are from Mars and Women from Venus*[13]) have been brought up by a society, at least in North America, that encourages us to avoid sharing emotions at all costs. We're supposed to be macho and strong and stoic and tough. Guys don't cry, and they don't share their feelings. The result is a high level of emotional illiteracy. The result is a "nation of boys who are hurting – sad, afraid, angry and silent.[14]" Funny, I don't ever remember feeling angry but, boy, was I ever sad, afraid, and very, very depressed. I didn't realize it at the time because I didn't want to. After all, I'm a man and men don't get scared, sad or depressed. That's being weak, or so I thought. Or so, as it turns out, I was brought up to think.

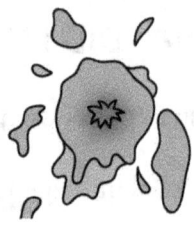

That was all about me. What about YOU?

What are you doing to make your journey of change EASYer on yourself? 😊 (or not ☹)?

What are some of your supporting characters?

_____

_____

_____

Are they a help or a hindrance?

_____

_____

Would it be okay if you invited them to move on?

_____

Is it possible there are better characters awaiting your company?

_____

Who might they be?

_____

_____

A ship in harbour is safe, but that is not what ships are built for.
William G.T. Shedd

PART 3
A Period of Pain in the Nasty Zone
(2009-2013)

ANXIETY & HELPLESSNESS
FAILURE
LONELINESS
FEAR
DEPRESSION
STUCK
LOW SELF-ESTEEM

Chapter 9:
Storm Clouds on the Horizon

You can't fall if you don't climb. But there's no joy in living your whole life on the ground.

Unknown

My DVD Collection

One of my tools for keeping my mind off my worries, my troubles, and my pain, was my DVD collection. I had 1,126 DVDs at last count. At an average viewing of 1.5 hours per day, they could keep my mind occupied and off my worries for years. In fact – a sad fact – 3.08 years, to be exact.

Spring 2009. Show Me the Money, if not the Meaning.

Once I had finally embarked upon my journey of success, the years started to tick away. My five-year work anniversary came and went quickly enough and then the big 1-0. Ten years! Not a whole lot of people work for the same employer for that long anymore. And before I knew it, I was coming up on 13 years. Thirteen years further along on my journey to success. That's a lot of years. Each of those years was represented by a row in the spreadsheet of the financial model I had developed. It was not a bad little model, if I do say so myself. It seamlessly integrated all of my financial assets and liabilities to give me the latest and greatest projections on how I was doing in meeting my goal of finding my freedom. Finding my freedom at age 55. There was one row for each year I had been with my employer, and it included my salary, bonus and performance rating for the year. Year after year. Promotion after promotion. Raise after raise. Bonus after bonus. Things were looking good on the financial front.

Both my wife and I had high-paying jobs, lots of savings and no debt. We were in the top percentile of the wealthiest people in Canada. And we only had about 11 years to go until we could ring the bell of Freedom 55. I could almost taste it. I had started out on my journey to success a little later than most, but I had done a pretty good job of catching up. Or so I thought. Little did I know at the time, but within a few years, my assets were going to drop overnight by 50%. My future earnings power was going to drop overnight by the same amount. The only thing that was not going to drop was my debt level. It was going to shoot up, and quite dramatically. It soon became "Bye-bye, Freedom 55" and "Hello, Divorce." But more on that later.

My career, meanwhile, had settled into a routine of annual performance targets, a series of raises, a potential bonus and an occasional promotion. I had pretty much advanced as far as I could, short of becoming a partner with the professional services firm I worked for, and I had ruled that option out from the get-go. There was no way I was going to work those kinds of hours and, besides, partners had to sell, and selling is not in my DNA. It never has been, and it never will be.

So, where was I heading back then? What were my goals? What did I want to be doing five years down the road? After all, I was 11 years from retirement, and that was still a fair way off. These were all good questions, but not the sort of questions I was asking myself. I was taking things one year at a time. One set of performance expectations, for one role, at a time. Was I heading in the right direction? Was I learning and growing? Again, these are good questions, but I didn't have any rows in my spreadsheet for those things. Besides, before I knew it, Freedom 55 would be upon me and I wouldn't have to worry about them. Or, so I thought. Or, so I thought until I came face to face with the dreaded "S" word. A word that was going to push me to the limits of my comfort zone.

Fall 2009. The Dreaded "S" Word. Can You Spell S-A-L-E-S?

Not thinking ahead on the career front was about to bite me in the ass. It turned out that, if I wanted to spend less time traveling and more time in my home city with the kids, I was going to have to start developing some expertise in areas other than in my main line of work, and fast. This was EASYer said than done. Especially since I had spent so long doing something I knew so well. How could I possibly be expected to turn on a dime?

Oh! And it was also time to start selling a few projects for my firm. After all, I was a senior manager and that was one of the expectations for the role. So far in my career, my level of technical experience and expertise had pretty much sold itself. I wasn't a salesperson. How was I now supposed to be able to both sell and deliver in a space where I had no experience? No experience, hence no comfort. After all, I had tried a sales role with another employer and that had not ended well. I basically walked away from that job. I had become so miserable that all I could think of doing to get out of that funk was to quit. Yes, quit. Fall on my sword. Hand in my resignation and put an end to the pain.

In those days, I had had no commitments and no kids. I was single, with no Freedom 55 plan to fund. But things were different now. I could look for something else, but I would never be able to find something that paid as well as the job I currently had, and we needed the money. Heaven forbid we drop below the top percentile on the wealth scale!

Things started heading south fast. I no longer wanted to travel but I couldn't find projects where travel was not a requirement. For me, that resulted in not doing a whole lot of work and, as I was going to find out in short order, that wasn't going to reflect well in my next annual performance review.

Fall 2009. "DP." Time to Shape up or Ship out. Call in the Coach, the "Sales Coach."

It was looking highly likely that I would receive a dreaded "DP" on my annual performance rating for the first time in close to 13 years of working for my employer. DP stands for Developmental Performance. Basically, it meant that it was time for me to shape up or ship out. That was the bad news. The good news was that my employer was ready to invest in me. I was assigned a new coach. A performance coach. In my case, part of my performance-related issue was my aversion to the word "sales." So, guess what? He was a sales performance coach. One of the best in the region. One of the most senior and most successful in the region. He actually loved the word "sales." I guess my employer was hoping that some of that love for sales would rub off on me. It turns out that their hopes were misplaced. Unfortunately for them, and for me, by the time they called in the cavalry, I was way too stuck in my comfort zone.

My new coach picked up on my love for my comfort zone quickly and implored me to get out…but I couldn't. I couldn't because I didn't believe I could. And I was scared. And what do I do when I'm scared? In those days, I would hide. I would hide in my basement with my DVDs. I would hide in the corner of the food court with my newspapers during my depression lunches. It turns out that others were ready to help me as well back then, but, unless I believed I could be helped, it was all for naught. A waste of everyone's time. Captain Courageous would have to wait. Captain Comfort Zone was not ready to leave the building, not yet, anyway, but he was getting close. Close to leaving because his "Comfort Zone" was starting to become his "Nasty Zone."

My Mid 40s. Eating More + Moving Less + Sleeping Even Less = Loss of Energy = Putting on the Pounds.

For someone who had never been overseas until he was well into his early thirties, I was catching up on my travel, and fast. Between my work travel and the resulting airmiles I accumulated, I was seeing a lot of the world. I was also collecting hotel points. Collecting lots of hotel points and eating lots of hotel food. Can you say "room service"? There's nothing better after a long day at work than to settle down in bed in front of the TV and order up the works. And by "the works," I mean an appetizer, a main course, a dessert and two drinks to wash it all down. And don't forget a bag of chips and a chocolate bar for a snack later in the evening. Yum. Such were my eating habits in those days, and they were habits that squeezed exercise into the minute or so it took to answer the door when room service knocked. My weight, you ask? In January 2011 at my heaviest I was 264 pounds.

Can you say obese? Can you say medicated? I needed a lot of pills to help me with my low good cholesterol levels and with my high bad cholesterol levels. Can you say pre-diabetic? I was not yet on diabetes-related medication but with the sugar in my diet from all the chocolates and desserts and booze I was consuming, I was well on my way to another prescription from my doctor. Can you say lack of energy? I had no energy to do anything but sit around all day. It was a good thing I had my movies and pots of coffee and lots of weekend football games to watch on TV. Go, Jets, go!

My Mid 40s. Hanging out in My Comfort Home. More Like Hiding out.

As I've mentioned, over the years I had created quite the comfort life for myself. It included a comfort home with several fridges full of comfort foods and comfort booze. It included more than 1,000 comfort movies. It included comfort projects around the house – I always seemed to have one underway. And let's not forget my Freedom 55 plan, my comfort dream that everything was going to be fine when I turned 55 and retired. When I left the comfort of my home, I had my mobile comfort zones ready and waiting. Comfort zone lunch hangouts in each of the cities where I traveled? Check! Comfort hotel rooms with room service in each of the cities where I traveled? Check! I had built or discovered a lot of comfort zones. I had developed a lot of comfort zone strategies and approaches and tools. Stitch them all together and I had quite the cross-country comfort network. Looking back, I realize I was quite the SME (Subject Matter Expert) in building and maintaining (and hiding in) comfort zones.

Things had gotten pretty scary for me in those days. I still remember pulling up to my home and how safe it made me feel. It was almost as if there was an impenetrable shield covering my house. I could actually see it when I turned the corner onto my street and saw my house. I was safe in my house. I was scared when I left. It got to where I just wanted to stay on my property all of the time. It really was my castle. My fortress of solitude. Little did I realize that I was building my own prison. Except for my children, it was becoming my prison of solitude. I was shutting out more and more people as each day passed. The more people I shut out, the nastier life became. The nastier it became, the more I wanted to hide. And things were getting very nasty. Freedom 55 was starting to look very far off. Was I ever going to make it? I had reached the point where I was checking off the days on the calendar. Checking off the days of my life. And there were still a lot of them left before I reached age 55. Or so I thought. Given the state of my health at the time, and my family's history of heart disease, I probably had fewer years left than I thought.

SO, WHAT DID I LEARN?

How did I make change EASYer on myself ☺ (or not ☹)?

In coaching, we talk about the importance of maintaining BOTH our personal and professional foundations. Maintaining a strong foundation is supposedly a great way of making it EASYer to take care of OURselves and others. Taking care of ourselves on the personal side of things includes such activities as eating healthily, getting enough sleep, hydrating well (with water, not booze), exercising enough, respecting ourselves, honouring ourselves, caring for ourselves, connecting with others, etc. Taking care of ourselves on the professional side of things includes continuous learning, growing, stretching, connecting with others, etc. In my case, in this phase of my life, I was not taking care of myself on either of those fronts. I was not taking care of my foundation and, hence myself, at all. ☹

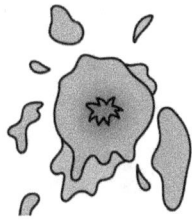

That was all about me. What about YOU?
What are you doing to make your journey of change EASYer on yourself?☺ (or not ☹)?

What zone are you spending most of your time in these days?

_____

_____

Is it serving you well? (Be honest, you're the only one who knows the answer, and the only one whose life is at stake here!)

_____

_____

Are you taking care of your personal foundation?

_____

_____

What healthy practice could you incorporate with little effort into your daily routine? (e.g. a 10-minute walk in the fresh air by day's end, etc.)

_____

_____

Chapter 10: Hitting the Wall and Getting Stuck

Faith is taking the first step even when you don't see the whole staircase.

Martin Luther King

The Road Warrior and a pretty chunky one! "Hello, room service? A large order of comfort food, please. Would I like dessert with that? Yes! Definitely! Maybe even two."

Stuck on the Career Front.
It Was Actually Much Broader than That.

In hindsight, I realize things had gotten pretty bad during what I now refer to as my "nasty time in my nasty zone." I thought that the nastiness was only career-related, but my troubles were much broader than that, much nastier than that. I would find that out a couple of years later the hard way but, fortunately for me at this point, I had finally reached the point where I was ready to start moving forward again – on the career front, if nowhere else. I would never recommend the approach I used to start moving forward, but at least it got me moving. Boy, was I ready to start moving forward! Moving forward could not be any worse than being stuck and absolutely miserable. I was discouraged. I had no energy. I no longer dreamed. I could no longer imagine what the future had in store for me, nor did I want to do that. I just wanted to be alone. I just wanted to hide and hope that all the nastiness around me would go away.

2009-2010 Overview. Stuck in What Turned out to Be My Clinical Depression Zone.

My recent Developmental Performance (DP) job rating was not the only "D" word I was wrestling with in those days. During that dark period of my life, it turns out I was also wrestling with a bout of depression – of the clinical variety. As I outlined in one of my blogs, aptly entitled "Let's talk about my bout with clinical depression"[15], I was diagnosed several years later when I finally decided to reach out and connect with some folks, including a mental health expert. I had no idea I was suffering from a mental illness. Since then, I have come across various studies that suggest that one in four or five Canadians (depends on the study) will experience mental illness along their life journey. That is 20%-25% of the Canadian population! My hypothesis is that there are similar rates in other countries. Yet the thought I might be one of them never occurred to me.

Very few thoughts crossed my mind in those days, though, and this was by design. As I've mentioned, I had pretty much isolated myself from everyone, including myself. My children were the exception to my isolationist strategy. If my kids had noticed signs of clinical depression in me, they didn't share those observations with me. Then again, how could they? We were hiding out watching so many movies together that there was no time for discussion. Besides, they were only five and three years old at the time and had yet to take any training on diagnosing clinical depression in one of their parents.

Perhaps my wife had noticed something but, in my efforts to avoid anything nasty, I had pretty much stopped thinking and talking about almost everything. I had stopped thinking and talking about almost everything with almost everyone, including my wife. With the exception of an occasional 90-minute date night, we had pretty much stopped talking altogether.

And things were getting worse at work. After a short break from traveling I was back on the road again. I couldn't avoid it. Local billable projects that suited my narrow skillset, not to mention mindset, were scarce and I hadn't worked on a billable project for much too long. There was just so much non-billable work that my employer was willing to invest in. My DP rating signaled the end of my travel moratorium. I became a road warrior again. When the alarm clock sounded on Monday mornings, off I went to the airport with my bags, plane tickets and a reservation for a "comfort" room at one of my favourite "comfort" hotels in hand. I would just have to see the kids on the weekends now.

On one trip, the project was not in my comfort zone. I had run out of my comfort-zone-type project options, so I had to bite the bullet on this one. Bite the bullet and smoke a couple of cigarettes. I was so stressed out on that project that I came up with a new daily ritual.

Every morning, just before arriving at the client site, I would inhale not one, but two cigarettes. And I mean inhale. No sooner had I lit up the first than I had finished inhaling and was lighting up the second.

Yes! Cigarettes. I was smoking about a pack and a half a week, and I had been for quite some time. It was my dirty little secret. A nasty secret for someone whose family has a history of heart disease and, as I had just recently discovered, someone who also now had a history of lung cancer in the family. As luck (or bad luck in this case) would have it, someone in my family had just been diagnosed with lung cancer, although, ironically, she had never been a smoker. She was my best friend, one of my closest confidants. She had been there for me my whole life. And she had been told that she had less than six months to live. She was my mom.

So much for seeing the kids on the weekends, at least not every weekend. For now, between client projects and hotel comfort rooms and cigarettes and lots of comfort food and comfort booze, I would be visiting my mom. I would be stopping by and visiting and watching her die slowly. Watching her die because watching was about all I could do in those days. I had stopped communicating. I had stopped feeling.

October 2009. If Misery Likes Company, Maybe Depression Does as Well.

Although I didn't know I was depressed at the time, my mom knew that she was. Something about knowing that you're dying can do that to you. She had medication to help her cope. She had her medication and I had mine (booze). My medicine was self-prescribed, hers was not. Understandably, the medication and the depression did not make her much of a conversationalist. Neither was I. I was aware of it, but

I wasn't sure why. I do now. I was so depressed, I wasn't aware of it. I remember just sitting there and staring at her. Not saying anything. Not thinking anything. Just staring at her. Staring at her as her life slipped by. Staring at her as my life slipped by. It would have been nice to have spent some quality time with her during the last days of her life but that was not to be. Although my body was physically there in the room with her, nothing else was. My head, my heart and my soul were all offline, and had been for some time.

March 2010. Time to Fall on My Sword. The Day the Pain Ended. On the Career Front, That Is.

Remember earlier I told you how I had been stuck in a nasty place on the job front once before? How I had ended that period of misery by falling on my sword? Well, guess what? Here I was, again, in a place where I had been almost 20 years previously. Stuck in a job that was not a fit. Feeling stressed, and miserable. Apparently, I also looked stressed and miserable. In this case, I was also clinically depressed. I was a functioning alcoholic. I was socially isolated. I was obese. I was in a terrible place, but I couldn't get out. I was stuck. A similar situation to being stuck in my previous job, except that now I had a family to support and it included two young children who I loved so much I would do anything for them. It was time to do something that had worked for me in the past and I hoped would work again. It was time to fall on my sword. Today was the day. I couldn't think of another option. And I couldn't go on this way. The pain had to stop. "I'm just going to do it," I thought. "I'm not going to tell my wife. I'm just going to do it. I'd rather beg for forgiveness later that night than ask for advice or permission beforehand."

I can't remember the exact date I took action. Wouldn't it be ironic if it were a Monday? I felt as though I had no other choice. We all have a choice, you say? Well, at the time, I saw my choice as staying and remaining stuck and miserable or quitting. Those were the possibilities open to David Arthur Walker on that day. At least in David Arthur Walker's mind. As seen through David Arthur Walker's lens. When you isolate yourself from other people, your lens, by extension, becomes the only lens. Just one lens. Not ideal for conjuring up a whole lot of possibilities…but I digress.

So, off went David Arthur Walker, off to see the Partner who had hired him into the firm more than 13 years previously, to let her know that he was done. He had given a lot to the firm over the years. He hoped that he had added value. He hoped that the time and value he had given to the firm would be taken into consideration when the HR folks decided what would be done with him. If not, he hoped that she and the firm would at least take pity on him. Pity was Plan B. Either way, it was time to go. I had spent enough time in that nasty, f**king, s**ty zone. It was time to just f**king move on.

As fate would have it, that Partner interrupted me as the words were coming out of my mouth. I forget exactly what she said, but it went something like this. "Dave, I've been thinking about you recently. You're not the same person I used to know. I think I've identified a possible solution. A new role for you. A new program. A new start. It's a temporary role I think you might like. Feel free to give it a try if you want to. I've arranged a one-hour meeting with the program leader in Toronto tomorrow. Plane tickets are waiting for you if you want to give it a try. . If you don't like it, at least it will give you a chance to look for something else." Wow. How cool is that?! How caring is that?

To make a long story short (I'll expand on the story in the next chapter), I did get on that plane the next day. I did accept the role. It took me a while to figure out what the role was all about (ironically enough, successfully transitioning into new roles was one of the program offerings). It took me a while to figure out what the program was all about. But figure it out, I did.

Within three years of that fateful meeting, for the first time in what would then be close to a 17-year career with the firm, I would receive an EP (Exceptional Performance) rating, the highest performance rating at the firm. I would receive an award from the global firm for my accomplishments in my new global role, a global role for one of the largest professional services companies in Canada and the world. This was a huge change on the job front! It was more of a transformation, from night to day. A transformation from feeling completely lost and discouraged to feeling engaged and energized. It was amazing!

Oh, and guess what? Regarding the dreaded "sales" word…within four years of the day I had decided to quit my job for the second time in my life, I had become the only non-partner in Canada to be asked to design and deliver a webinar as part of a national webinar series on, you guessed it, SELLING! And when it came time to reach out to facilitators to help deliver a new sales training to the partners and senior managers in Canada, guess who was the only person without a business development role who was asked to become part of the facilitation team? You guessed it. ME. Yes, little-old-crawl-under-a-table-at-the-mere-mention-of-the-word-sales ME. What a change!

SO, WHAT DID I LEARN?

How did I make change EASYer on myself ☺ (or not ☹)?

I've started using a tool that I refer to as my four "Life Quadrants." Why four? The number just seems to work for me. I equate it to juggling balls. Juggling three balls is hard enough for me at times. Four seems manageable, but I dare not press my luck by adding a fifth. I will cover the quadrants in more detail as we move forward but, suffice to say, when it comes to making change, I've found that I make it much EASYer on myself ☺ by focusing on one issue at a time. One next step, in one Life Quadrant at a time. One day at a time. And, when the going gets really tough, one minute at a time.

In this case, my focus was on my career quadrant. My one next step in this quadrant was to change roles, even if that meant quitting my job. Trying to tackle too much change at once and I was asking for trouble. As a former colleague of mine recently shared with me, there are so many variables that can come into play when making a change. Things can become overly complex and quite scary and discouraging pretty quickly. Paralysis from analysis is lurking just around the corner. Luckily for me I was able to stay focused during this period. Good thing, too, because I would soon become aware of other changes I would have to deal with – whether I wanted to or not.

Oh, and when it comes to making change, surrounding yourself with people who believe and respect and trust in you? Priceless! ☺

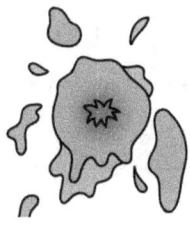

That was all about me. What about YOU?

What are you doing to make your journey of change EASYer on yourself? ☺ (or not ☹)?

Who could you surround yourself with – who believes and trusts in you?

_____

_____

Have you been in a situation (job, relationship, etc.) where you wanted out but couldn't see a way to extricate yourself?

_____

_____

How did you deal with it?

_____

_____

_____

Are you in a similar situation now?

_____

_____

What's one action you can take that will help you see if there are other possibilities you may not have envisioned yet?

_____

_____

_____

And what's one step you can take to help you move on?

_____

_____

_____

_____

Chapter 11:
Finding My Fit and a Bit of Self-Confidence

If you want to conquer fear, don't just sit at home and think about it. Go out and get busy.

Dale Carnegie

Assume the Position (My Depression Position)

This is a photo of me on my couch. This was my favourite hang-out spot when I was feeling down (depressed). What I liked most about my couch was that it allowed me to lie down. In those times of despair, I didn't have the energy to sit up.

May 2010. Time to Reconnect with Me and My Passions. Well, at Least It Was Time to Start.

I didn't know what I didn't know. That pretty much summed up where my head was at on that day in Toronto when I met with the partner whose program I was about to join.

- Was this what I was looking for to get me out of my career rut?
- Was this going to help me relaunch my career?
- Was this job going to allow me to play to my strengths?
- Was I going to find or rediscover my passion?
- Was I going to find my purpose?
- Was I going to stop dreading getting up in the morning? Especially Monday mornings!

These were pretty powerful questions that I might have been considering at this point, but I was not in a questioning state of mind. I was in a just-trying-to-get-by-in-life state of mind. I didn't know what I was looking for. I was having trouble just getting out of bed in the morning. Just being able to function was the only strength I was playing to.

My purpose? My passion? My long-term career aspirations? I had no clue. Have you ever tried the visioning exercise where you try to envision what things will look and feel like in three to five years? I couldn't even look six months ahead, let alone five years. The future was blank. And this from someone who would later identify "futuristic" as one of his top five strengths. "Futuristic: Inspired by the future and what could be."[16] Wow! And to think that, in those days, my future was inspired by my Freedom 55 plan. Hide from life until I turned 55 was the sum total of my plan. Somewhere I had lost my way. And along with losing my way, I had lost my confidence. I had lost my confidence and my belief and trust in myself. I had just spent the better part of my career aligning myself with a set of pre-defined generic performance standards. So much for playing to my strengths. I didn't even know what my strengths were. They seemed unimportant. It was all about exceeding the performance standards.

The generic, one-size-fits-all performance standards that seemed so important to my employer and me at the time. I spent so much time following a performance framework developed for a specific role that I had forgotten what made me tick as a person. Before I knew it, I no longer had any passion for what I was doing, and I was doing those things for 50-60 hours a week. Yuck!

But back to that day in May. Back to that one-hour meeting with the program leader in Toronto. It turned out to be a pretty one-sided conversation because I didn't understand what the program was all about. He spent an hour explaining it to me, but I was so clueless I couldn't come up with an intelligent question at the end of his description of the program. I couldn't come up with a single question, but I had an answer. "Yes," I responded when asked if I was interested, "I would like to join your program." Even though I didn't understand the role, and that lack of understanding placed me outside my comfort zone, I felt I had nothing to lose by giving it a try. Having no clue about what I wanted to do didn't inspire a lot of options. And besides, although I didn't trust myself a whole lot in those days, I trusted this leader and I was inspired by his passion for the program. And I trusted the person who had sent me to see him in the first place. So, I accepted the role.

Was it a good fit? Good question. It took me a while to figure that one out. It actually took me a few months to even figure out what the program was all about. But when I did, I started to find my passion. More like "feel" it. Feeling it turned out to be the way that I found it. I started to discover my likes and dislikes and I started to use them to shape my role and priorities. I started to find my strengths and I started to play to them. Before I knew it, my six-month secondment had become a permanent role that lasted five years; five of the most engaging and fulfilling years of my career; five years during which I grew so much that, when it was time to move on to my next career adventure, I was ready. No falling on my sword. No slinking away. I had found my confidence. I believed in myself. I trusted myself. When it came to making the next career transition – one of the biggest and boldest and most courageous career transitions of my life at an age when most people are slowing down, not gearing up – I was ready.

I'll tell you more about that big, bold, courageous transition in a later chapter but, for now, let's get back to reconnecting with myself back in those early days. How did I find my fit? How did I find (or rediscover) my confidence? It was pretty straightforward. I tried a lot of things. A lot of things. Some of the things fit and some did not but, the more I tried, the more I got to know myself and what felt comfortable to me, and what did not. The funny thing was that the things I didn't think I'd like, I ended up liking, and vice-versa. It was as if I was making the theory real by trying it out. It was like trying to find a pair of shoes that fit properly. A pair of shoes that fit snugly. How do you do that? Well, you try them on for size. You put them on and walk around a bit. I can't tell you how nice it felt to finally start wearing a pair that fit. My previous pair had been quite painful, actually – more like very, very painful.

Oh, and what about the performance standards for that role? It turns out there were none. I was given the opportunity to shape my own role. I was given the opportunity to explore how I could best contribute to the program. If trying things out was the way to find my fit, I had my chance. Carte blanche. No hand-holding. It was up to me to shape my own role. Apparently, not only did I trust the leader of the program, but he also trusted me. He trusted me to figure out how I could add the most value to the program. How I could best meet the program mission and objectives. There's nothing like a vote of confidence from someone else to help you find your self-confidence, especially when yours is at an all-time low.

It took me a while to figure things out. A lot of things did not go as planned. I learned a lot of lessons, but guess what? I shaped and discovered things by doing. It took me a while to build up the courage to start doing; after all, I was Captain Comfort Zone, not Captain Courageous in those days. I found that the more I ventured out of my comfort zone, the more I learned, and the more my self-confidence grew, and the more I wanted to venture out to try even more new things. To get to know myself even more. Before I knew it, I had built up some serious momentum, and along with that momentum came more courage and more exploring. A friend of mine likes to refer to the magic of the momentum-building process as the "ripple effect." In this case, it was a positive ripple effect. And it was a nice change from the negative ripple effects I had been experiencing. This one had a positive impact on my level of engagement and the resulting level of my self-confidence, courage, and, ultimately, trust. Trust in myself, something I had lost a while back.

Ironically, the program I joined was about developing trusted business advisors. It was about helping others develop confidence and trust in themselves, so they could develop and maintain relationships of trust. I can't speak for the others, but it certainly worked for me. It took a while to regain that trust in myself. A lot of learning and a lot of doing, but isn't that how we learn? By doing? After all, we don't know what we don't know. Until we try it.

November 2011. Time to Reconnect with Others. It Turns out That Passion Is Contagious.

Directing a program required connecting with people. It was time to start reaching out and, since this was a global program, it was time to start reaching out to a lot of people. Reaching out and connecting with people hadn't been among my top priorities during my social isolation days. Social isolation strategies by definition do not involve reaching out, and I did a pretty good job of executing on that strategy. Besides, I'm the "shy guy," so reaching out isn't in my comfort zone; especially if I don't know the other person. Many of these people were in very senior positions, which I found quite intimidating.

So, how did I do it? I just did it. I started to reach out to some of my peers and leaders of the program in other countries. And guess what? Not only did they get back to me, they actually seemed to enjoy exchanging ideas and insights with me. In addition to our desire to exchange insights and ideas, we had a couple of other things in common. One was a sense of passion for the program, as well as a sense of purpose. It was contagious. And it was incredibly motivating. Maybe it was my imagination, but it seemed like everyone had been drinking the program's Kool-Aid – for a long time. Suddenly, my fear of reaching out to new people was being replaced by the excitement of meeting new people. And, since my role was global, that meant meeting people from all over the world!

I was finally waking up excited to start my day. I had come a long way. I had a lot of people to thank for helping me make that happen, including myself for having the courage to, well, just do it. From falling on my sword to trying things out to just plain old reaching out. I was just doing it. I met a lot of really great people. In his book on finding happiness, *The Happiness Equation*, Neil Pasricha puts forward his theory that "you are the average of the five people around you." [17] Apparently, I was hanging around the right crowd.

January 2012. Time to Start Taking Better Care of Myself.

Although I was finally starting to gain some positive energy on at least one front in those days (the career front), I still wasn't taking care of myself on the health front. I was not moving (exercising) enough. I was eating too much – and too much of the wrong stuff. I was drinking too much of the wrong stuff (yes, the booze was still flowing). I was going to bed too late and not getting enough sleep.

What I lacked in sleep I more than made up for in coffee, and my late nights were still being aided and abetted by a bottle of wine. In my haste to start working on something that finally resonated with me, I would often miss out on some of my meals. I liked to brag about it at the time. For some reason, I thought that I was being super-productive. I even came up with my own words for what I was doing. "Brrcrunch" was what I called it when I consumed both my breakfast and lunch at the same time. "DinnerBrrcrunch" was when I consumed breakfast, lunch and dinner all at the same time at my desk while working. I believe they call that multi-tasking.

It was going to take me a little while longer to realize that my approach to increasing my productivity via multi-tasking was not the healthiest choice, and I was not as productive as I thought. As a matter of fact, it was quite the opposite. Oh! And to top it all off, I had hit the 264-pound mark about a year earlier. That was the heaviest I had ever been in my life.

At least there was some good news on the health front. After many seemingly futile and short-lived attempts to stop smoking, I finally quit cold-turkey. I was at a truck stop for lunch one day enjoying a post-lunch cigarette when a thought occurred to me, "What would my kids do, how would they feel if I died from a heart attack or lung cancer?" I'm not sure if I came up with an answer, but that cigarette was the last cigarette I would smoke. Talk about a motivator! Thanks, kids! I may be getting ahead of myself here, but the kids were going to come to my rescue again on the health front in the not-too-distant future, but more on that in a later chapter.

Getting Unstuck, at Least on One Front. Talk about Good Timing!

When I look back on those painful days when I was stuck on the career front, I sometimes wonder what would have happened if I had come out of that rut earlier. I also wonder what would have happened if I had come out of that rut, heaven forbid, later, or maybe never.

As advocates of "being in the moment" like to point out, what is in the past is in the past. So, I won't dwell on the past, but I am grateful I finally got around to making and building on that change. Not only did it have a profound impact on my career path later on, but my decision to move forward, with the support of others and not just by myself, allowed me to get back on my feet and gain some much-needed energy, more self-confidence and, of course, more courage. As it turned out, I was going to need all the energy and courage I could lay my hands on for what was going to happen to me in the next chapter of my life. For what was going to happen to me and my family. More like my new life, my new life as a single parent.

SO, WHAT DID I LEARN?

How did I make change EASYer on myself ☺ (or not ☹)?

Ever hear the term "playing to one's strengths"? The theory is that you can make things EASYer on yourself by focusing on what YOU, as a unique individual, both do well and enjoy doing. Kind of a "Top 5" list. Not only have I heard the term, but I have taken the time required to flush them out. I have my Top Five Strengths posted next to me on my office wall. I swear by them. I honour them. I don't know what I did before I embraced them.

But back in the bad, old nasty days, I didn't have a handle on my strengths or what made me tick. My self-awareness levels were low. Everyone likes to feel as if they're contributing, yet I didn't know how I was adding value. I knew what scared me and what made me anxious (almost everything new in those days), but I was in the dark about what really excited and energized me. Instead of taking a proactive approach by exploring the things I liked to do, and the people I liked to do them with, I was in total reactive mode. I was sitting around (more like lying around), waiting for good things to happen to me and I was becoming disillusioned, discouraged and eventually depressed when they did not. ☹

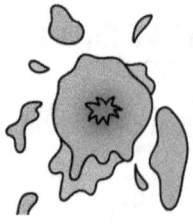

That was all about me. What about YOU?
What are you doing to make your journey of change EASYer on yourself? ☺ (or not ☹)?

Does your job allow you to play to your strengths?

_____

_____

If the answer is "no," can you see a way to change your role to allow you to do that?

_____

_____

Who are the five people you are spending the most time with?

_____

_____

What's the 'brand' of the collective five? Positive?

_____

_____

Chapter 12: Another Shoe Falls

All relationships have one law. Never make the one you love feel alone, especially if you're there.

Unknown

March 2012. Speaking of Partners, We're Not Spending a Lot of Time Together. Is that Really the Norm?

I had been spending a lot of time with partners at my place of work. As one of the largest professional services firms in the world, there were a lot of partners to spend time with. But there was another partner at that time in my life and I was not spending a lot of time with her. That partner was my life partner, my wife. From the outset of our life together, my business travel had been part of our regular routine, but the amount of away-time was increasing, and I seemed to be away more, even when I was not traveling. Our routine started to change when the kids were born. It was tough finding time to spend as a couple when we were both working, maintaining the house, and keeping up with the weekly run-of-the-mill to-do's, etc., but when kids were added to the mix, something had to give. Or so I thought.

In our case, what seems to have given way was our time together. It started with the birth of our son and, then, really took hold when my daughter arrived a couple of years later. With two young children to manage, our idea of a balanced lifestyle (or at least my idea of one) was to divide and conquer: I would tackle some family tasks with my son, and my wife would tackle others with my daughter. Then we would switch kids. That was how we seemed to balance our time between work and chores and combine it all with time with the kids. We would throw in a little time with the whole family and some time with our extended family. Whatever time was left at the end of the day was for the two of us. And it wasn't much. Most of our together time was of the end-of-the-day variety, when we were both tired. Our together time turned into a ritual of watching a DVD or a TV show. There was a lot of watching, but not much talking.

The word "tired" also summed up how I felt on our sporadic date nights; sporadic because I was tasked with organizing them and, when that task came up on my to-do list, I was so tired that just booking something required monumental effort. So, I often didn't make any plans and our dates became even more hit or miss. When I did plan them, I was so tired that they often ended early. "Okay, we've eaten. Should we get going now? Big day tomorrow and we still need to put the kids to bed!" Not much of a date! Throw in my bout of depression and the accompanying isolationist, non-conversational behaviour, and our quality time together really dried up to the point of non-existence.

If my wife's love language included quality time, we were in trouble. Mine didn't include quality time because I didn't have any. I was in such a far-off place I didn't even notice. I wasn't aware of the neglect and pain I was causing. I wasn't aware of the pain I was feeling. That was part of the problem that came from ignoring my feelings – I no longer felt them. Eventually I no longer felt anything.

I didn't realize that I had checked out of our relationship, despite my wife's occasional attempts to bring up the topic. She would broach the subject in the form of a question, "Is it just me or does it seem like we're not spending a lot of time together?" To that, I would answer, "Don't worry, it's normal. We both have demanding jobs, we have the kids, the house and all that comes with those responsibilities. Hang in there. Freedom 55 isn't that far away. We'll have lots of time to spend together then." I'd bring up the TV ads for European river tours. "We'll catch up on one of those cruises," I would tell her, "with a glass of wine in our cabin on the boat." Her retort to that was, "Aren't those boats filled with old people?" Hmmm. I guess they were. I guess we'll just have to wait until we're old to spend quality time together. And our marriage vows – to love, honour and cherish one another – I guess that will have to wait as well. Wait until we have more time, more quality time.

After numerous inquiries from my wife on the subject of our spending less and less time together, I decided to ask someone else to share their thoughts on the subject. Yes, my wife had been so persistent that I decided I needed some objective input to validate my "everything's normal" assertion. But just this once. My approach was to ask another man, another "Martian." I realize now that it might have been prudent to connect with a few citizens from the planet Venus as well, but I did not. And the feedback from my fellow Martian? It went something like this, "That's normal. My wife and I don't see much of each other, either. Our jobs, school for the kids, sports for the kids, activities for the kids, etc. It doesn't leave much time for us as a couple."

Okay, things couldn't be that bad if others were going through the same thing. I guess we'll have a lot of company on those European cruises. Sounds like a lot of people will have a lot of catching up to do once their careers wind down and the kids move out. Until then, we'll just have to bite the bullet. Or so I thought until the night another shoe fell. The night my marriage ended.

This chart depicts what I am calling My Personal and Professional Balanced Scorecard. It has four Life Quadrants. At this stage of my life journey, there was going to be a major vacancy in one of them. ☹

My Personal and Professional Balanced Scorecard
(a.k.a. My FOUR LIFE Quadrants) Where do I want to focus my time and energy?

Family and Friends		Business and Career	
Vacation time	Soccer dad	Learn and Grow (L&G)	Flexibility
Quality time	Movie time		Impact
BBQ time	Hike	Alignment with values	Fun & Funding
Fun time	Connect		Share & care
Holiday time	Leisure	Autonomy	Collaboration

Center: Values, Strengths, Preferences, Priorities

SOULMATE		ME, Myself and I	
Date nights	Hiking	Treadmill	Cook
1-on-1 time	Soccer dad	Fun Gym	Read
Love	Movie time	Rollerblade	Movie night
Staring in each	Connecting	Re-energize	Rest &
other's eyes	Leisure time	L&G	Relaxation

CURRENT VACANCY (overlaid on SOULMATE quadrant)

108 MONDAYS *don't have to* SUCK!

There are only so many hours in a day. Only so many days in our lifetime. Where do I want to spend mine? What about you?

A Friday Night in February 2013. Another Shoe Falls.

It was a good thing I had finally decided to make some changes on the career front. It was a good thing I was feeling better. And by feeling better, I mean, not feeling depressed. Luckily for me, I had overcome my period of clinical depression and was moving forward on the job front. I was gaining energy from that positive momentum. That was a good thing, because things were going to take another turn for the nasty. Another type of nasty.

After a little more than 10 years of marriage, I was about to become a single parent. So much for the Freedom 55 plan. I guess the periodic date nights didn't work after all. It was time to update my financial spreadsheet. Time to drop by the bank to see if I could take out a mortgage on a house. Time to figure out how to tell the kids. Time to figure out how to tell the family. And, let's not forget, it was time for me to figure out what had happened. Was that what marriage was all about? It sounded like everyone and everything else took priority over "the couple." At least that seemed to be how I had been trying to make it all work. And apparently that wasn't working all that well for me or my wife – my soon-to-be-ex-wife.

That period of contemplation would have to wait until a later time. As I will explain in the next chapter, I soon realized I had some other priorities to deal with. Not dying was one of them. Not dying was going to take most of my focus and energy for the next couple of years and, until I had that one under control, I would put a hold on tackling my "Soulmate Quadrant."

My "Soulmate Quadrant" is one of the four Life Quadrants on "My Personal and Professional Balanced Scorecard," which wasn't all that balanced in those days. Given my recent change in marital status, I made the conscious decision to focus on two of my other Life Quadrants, my "Me, Myself and I Quadrant" and my "Family and Friends Quadrant," with the main focus on the latter quadrant, which included my kids. And remember, I still had to keep my eye on the ball in my "Career Quadrant" so as not to lose my new-found momentum. I would be juggling three balls (quadrants) at once. I didn't want to push my juggling skills too far by taking on a fourth. Not yet. My soulmate would have to wait.

My children were nine and seven years old by this time. Their lives and routines were about to undergo a major change and I wanted to spend more time with them during that transition. Finding or rediscovering love would have to wait until later on. Finding my soulmate would have to wait. Who knows, maybe I would meet her on one of those European canal cruises? That might be a bit late in the game, but better late than never. In the meantime, I had other priorities.

Another Transition. Two actually. To Single Parent and Co-Parent.

It was a good thing that I was in no rush on the soulmate front because I had my hands full on the parenting transition front. I didn't realize it at first, but I was about to undertake two transitions, not just one. Two transitions for the price of one. Two new roles. Two new changes to make in my life. That was a tall order for anyone, but I wasn't just anyone. I was (still) Captain Comfort Zone, and I already had enough change going on in my career quadrant to keep me busy, thank you very much.

The first transition I had to navigate was to single-parent status and, given my physical appearance and feelings of negative self-esteem in those days, I felt I was likely to remain single for quite some time. This transition was an obvious one: One day I was married and living with my wife and the mother of my children, and, the next day, I was not. I was single. I was a single parent. Our "new normal" took some getting used to for all those affected, but we managed to move on with our lives. But looking back on those sad days, what really made a difference was just how supportive my family and friends were. As it turned out, my divorce was one of the catalysts that allowed me to reconnect with my family and friends after that dark period of shutting everyone out. Boy, did I feel blessed! Remind me not to shut them out again. Lesson learned! I should be connecting with people during tough times, not shutting them out.

The second transition was not as obvious, not at first, anyway. The second transition was in my role as a parent. I was now becoming a co-parent. At first, I took on the role of being "Super Dad." Not only was Super Dad able to do things that a dad could and should do, he could also do the things that a mom could and should do. As it turned out, the dad-things were EASYer than the mom-things. I never did figure out how to braid hair but, before long, I realized I didn't have to. Luckily for me and the kids, I realized there was a role and a need for a mom in their lives, and there was a role and a need for a dad. Instead of trying to be both Mom and Dad, my time would be better spent working on my skills as Super Co-Parent. EASYer said than done. It takes the courage and confidence of both co-parents to make this work and, as you know, courage wasn't a strong point for me in those days. My motivator was, and still is, my two beautiful children. It doesn't get any more motivating than that!

SO, WHAT DID I LEARN?

How did I make change EASYer on myself ☺ (or not ☹)?

Why is it that, when it comes to maintaining work-life balance, the couple always seems to come last? Or is that just my impression? We read a lot these days about the importance of taking care of oneself, which, as I will explain shortly, is not only very important, but crucial, but I rarely see or hear anyone advocating the importance of making time for the couple. Real quality couple time! Come Hell or high water! They say that 50% of marriages end in divorce. The statistics are even worse for second marriages. And don't forget all of the couples who are legally married and/or living as a couple but, for all intents and purposes, have a relationship that has already ended.

In his book, *The Five Love Languages: The Secret to Love that Lasts*[18], author Gary Chapman makes the case for not only being aware of your partner's love language, but actually making time to play to it. As he puts it, "The number of ways to express love within a love language, is limited only by your imagination." So, not only should I be making things EASYer on myself by honouring and playing to my strengths, but I should also be doing the same when it comes to my love language and that of my soulmate. Or, at this time of my life, my future soulmate. ☹

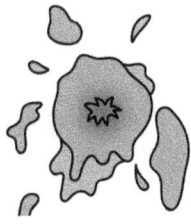

That was all about me. What about YOU?
What are you doing to make your journey of change EASYer on yourself? ☺ (or not ☹)?

How are things on the soulmate front?

_____

_____

Do you know your partner's love language?

_____

_____

Are you speaking each other's love language?

_____

_____

And, if so, are you both speaking it often enough?

_____

_____

Chapter 13: Grabbing the Oxygen Mask!

Taking good care of you means the people in your life will receive the best of you, rather than what's left of you.

Carl Bryan

Whenever I think of this stage of my life journey, I picture the oxygen masks that fall from above the passenger seats in an airplane and the airline instructions on the proper use of the oxygen mask: Put your oxygen mask on yourself first, before helping others.

The Day the Oxygen Mask Fell.

It was like cigarette-quitting time all over again. I mentioned that, after several half-hearted (and, therefore, ultimately futile) attempts to quit smoking, I had done it cold-turkey. It was a spur-of-the-moment decision. It came out of the blue. A sudden realization came to me as I was puffing away on a cigarette: I was increasing the odds, exponentially, that, if I did not quit, my children would grow up without a father. Why that day and not some other day? I don't know. I had been aware of the risks of smoking for a long time. Pictures on cigarette packages were quite graphic in those days. The evidence was plain to see. Yet I chose not to. Maybe I figured that nothing bad would happen to me. Well, whatever it was that made me finally see the light on that particular day and, more importantly decide to act on it, it happened again, on another day, not once, but twice.

My smoking days were behind me. Now my 15 plus years (or 5,475 days) of being overweight were about to come to an end as well. Another day had now arrived when my kids would come to my rescue. Once again, I had come to realize that the odds of me dying and leaving my children without a father were – well, let's just say – right up there. It was time for another lifestyle change. If I couldn't do it for myself, what about doing it for them? That was my first thought. The first shoe dropped. Then the second shoe fell, and good thing it did. I was going to need both of them along the journey I was about to embark upon, and that journey was picking myself up and moving on with my life. Moving on, but on a much more fulfilling path.

May 2013. Looking in the Mirror and Not Liking Who Was Looking Back at Me!

The first shoe drops. "Hey, buddy, keep it up and your children won't have a father much longer." I don't remember the exact date, but I still remember the day as if it were yesterday. That day, I had gotten out of bed like every other day and, just like every other day, that meant looking at myself in the mirror. I have mirrors on the closet doors in my bedroom so, like it or not, I get to see a lot of myself, and often.

And although I didn't like what was looking back at me in those days, I had gotten used to it.

Sure, I had tried to lose weight on a few occasions over the years. I bought a treadmill. I bought an exercise bike. I bought a bunch of other health-related gadgets. I can't remember a New Year's resolution that didn't include some new type of exercise equipment. Although most quickly found a new home, compliments of the local annual community garage sale, I still had my treadmill. It was in the basement gathering dust. A sad reminder of what happens when I try to get in shape. A reminder to stop wasting my time and money on lost causes. I should know better by now. I tried it, often, and it didn't work. Time to accept it. I was a lot older now and wiser (48 years wiser and weighing in at 238 pounds back then, a BMI of close to 30). I knew better than to waste my money and time on things that just didn't work. Time to make peace with myself. I am who I am. Accept it.

With that in mind, I started to get used to seeing that dude in the mirror. I got used to seeing him, day in and day out. He was not the healthiest-looking guy. He was not the handsomest guy either. Especially lately. He had started to shave his head, figuring it would dry quicker and, at $10 a pop, it was quite cost-effective. And the choice of clothes. Same strategy. Buy them on the cheap. No point in trying to look good if you don't feel good. Just make sure they're size XL. I was an accountant, not a fashion model. You know what? If this is what it's come to, so be it. I can live with myself. I can live with my looks. I can live with my feelings (my feelings of low self-worth). I was even making it EASYer on myself to do so in those days. I was making it a habit. A ritual. A daily ritual. Looking in that mirror had become a daily reminder that I had given up on life.

For some reason, on this particular day I looked in that mirror and suddenly it struck me: I cannot live this life. I cannot live this lifestyle. I'm obese. I'm taking medication everyday to control my cholesterol levels, both of which are out of whack; I'm self-medicating with booze; and I'm pre-diabetic. My grandfather had had a heart attack and died around this age. He left three young sons, one of whom was my father, who also had a heart attack, and at an even younger age.

"Well, you know what, buddy?" I thought to myself. "Keep this up and you're going to have a heart attack, too, unless you change the way you're living. You're going to have a heart attack and die. You're going to die and leave your children without a father. F**K YOU! Get your F**CKING act together! Starting now!" Talk about a motivator! Not dying. If not for myself, then I to had do it for them. By them, I meant the kids. My kids. My two beautiful kids.

The Second Shoe Falls. Hey, Buddy, Isn't It about Time You Started Living?

Within a few seconds of my deciding to do something about my health, or lack thereof, the second motivator came in to play. What I call a double-tap. Double-tap was the recommended approach to killing zombies in the movie "Zombieland." It was a way of increasing the odds that zombies stayed dead. I was going to use this approach, too, to increase the odds I would not end up like the zombies–dead. I was so tired of feeling like I was among the living dead. The living who had given up on living.

I was going to use not one motivator but two, my kids and me. So, I looked at that guy in the mirror, I looked him straight in the eyes and I told him. "Buddy, your days of giving up on life are over! Your days of settling for less are over! You're going to turn things around! I don't know how you're going to do it but do it you will!" Wow! What took me so long?

F**k the Soulmate Quadrant, for Now. Time to Circle the Wagons and Reconnect with Family.

So much for worrying about filling my dance card in my now-vacant soulmate quadrant. I could only see three oxygen masks at that moment, two for the kids and one for me, and that's all I felt I could juggle at the time. Speaking of time, it was time to do something I hadn't done in a while, and that was take care of myself. It had been so long I had almost forgotten how to do it.

I also wanted to spend more time with the kids during what would likely be a very difficult period of their life journeys. It was time to circle the wagons. And while I was circling them, it might not be a bad idea to reconnect with my family. A little extra support from my family might come in handy right about now. Well, guess what? I never did get the chance. I never got the chance to reach out to them because they beat me to it. They reached out to me. The calls started coming in the minute they heard about my new single status. Calls and visits and the energy that comes from spending time with others. I was so grateful. Talk about healthy lifestyle changes! In addition to moving more and eating better, I might want to spend a little more time connecting with others as well. Bye-bye, isolation. Good riddance!

SO, WHAT DID I LEARN?

How did I make change EASYer on myself 😊 (or not ☹)?

Change starts with YOU. It takes time and it takes effort. In the end, it's YOUR choice to undertake change or not. It's YOUR choice to grab the oxygen mask or not. So, when the time for change beckons, especially change of a more daunting kind, and the oxygen mask comes down, you might want to make that change EASYer on yourself by grabbing that oxygen mask and strapping it on. If not for YOU, then for those who are depending on YOU to make that change happen, and to make it stick. And while you are strapping it on, surrounding yourself with family, friends and colleagues who care about YOU does not hurt either. 😊

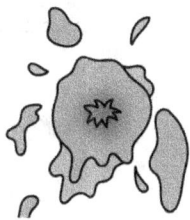

That was all about me. What about YOU?

What are you doing to make your journey of change EASYer on yourself? ☺ (or not ☹)?

If you are looking at making a change in your life, what is your catalyst to make that change happen, and then to maintain it moving forward?

_____

_____

What is going to happen to you and those you care about if you don't make any changes? Where is that train heading?

_____

_____

Who can you recruit to be on your support team to make a significant change?

_____

_____

What if you could make your life 1% better every month? In a year that's well more than a 10% improvement. What would a 10% improvement in your life feel like?

_____

_____

*You are entering the transition zone, Mr. Walker.
Which way will it be?*

PART 4
Finding the *Real* Me
(2013-2016)

Chapter 14: Finding My FIT-ness Routine

*Take care of your body.
It is the only place you have to live.*

Jim Rohn

A picture of the physical results of "My f**k the No Pain, No Gain" approach to getting healthier. I was getting healthy and having fun doing it! These are the roller-blades that got me going.

July 2017. MOVE. EAT. DRINK. SLEEP. LOVE. A New Formula. Making It EASYer on Myself.

This month marks the one-year anniversary of sharing my second-ever blog, "Dave's Top 5 List: How I lost close to 100 pounds of body fat."[19] Although the initial motivator for making a change in my life and my lifestyle was to "not die" and leave my kids without a father, I found that, once I started making progress on the health-and-wellness front, the results surpassed my wildest dreams. It was incredible how

I turned so many bad health habits into good ones. Before I knew it, I was buying a whole new wardrobe. I had dropped close to 100 pounds of body fat as a by-product of changing my ways and, unlike most people who lose weight (by some counts 90%), I had kept it off for well more than a year. The weight has stayed off and the healthy habits that keep it off have remained.

In the first part of "my losing weight" blog and in the first chapters of this book, I share how I had put on the weight. It took me years to put it on and my weight yo-yoed but, in the end, I had developed a bunch of nasty habits that helped maintain my nasty weight and lifestyle. I even shared my magic formula in my blog, "Eat crap. Lots of It. Often. Drink crap. Lots of it. Often. Don't exercise. Ever." This is my "nasty health-zone formula." In that same blog, I also share my formula for taking off the weight, and keeping it off. Weight loss was not my primary goal but a by-product of changing my ways – changing unhealthy ways to healthy ways and adding healthy habits to maintain those healthy ways. My formula was simple: "Eat healthy. Drink in moderation. Exercise frequently. Enjoy." What did I call this formula? I dropped the word "nasty" and added a "y" to "health." And, voilà, I had my "healthy-zone formula."

Over the last year, I've had time to try more things and I think it's time to update the formula. The original name was inspired by a book by Tom Rath called *Eat, Move, Sleep*.[20] I really enjoyed reading that book. It has lots of ideas to pick and choose from. Some worked for me and some didn't. Remember, my approach is to make things EASYer on myself and have fun doing it, so any idea in that book that didn't pass that quick test was quickly rejected. The formula I came up with became a "Top Five List: MOVE. EAT. DRINK. SLEEP. LOVE." Here's the story behind my new, simplified "healthy-zone formula." Remember, this was about my health and my level of energy. It doesn't get more important than that.

May 2013. MOVE More. Finding My Rollerblades and Dusting Them off.

Some would argue that "eat" should come before "move" in the grander scheme of things, especially regarding weight loss, which would support the order the author chose for the words in the title, *Eat. Move. Sleep.* Well, guess what? Since this is my book and my life-transformation, I'm starting with "move," although "eat" was a close second and was to follow very shortly thereafter; in fact, only by a matter of days for those who are counting.

The first step toward moving more turned out to be my first skate, my first roller-skate on my rollerblades. It had been so long since I had exercised that I had forgotten how to do it. So, once I decided that I would just try and do something that would get me to move, my biggest question was to find that one thing as an immediate next step. One thing to try. What could that be?

I decided that the best way to find my fit while making it EASYer on myself at the same time was to try something that was both easy and fun to do. And that's just what I did. I dug out my rollerblades and dusted them off. The very next day, I put them on and went around the block. Once around the block became twice around the block and, then, once around the neighbourhood. Then I decided to dust off my bike, pump up the tires and start pedalling. Every once in a while, I would take the stairs instead of the escalator. Then I came up with the idea of joining a gym. A while after the idea arrived, I joined. A while after that, I actually went. A pattern was emerging. I was starting to move. Hitting the gym, but not hard. I'm still a member today. I still rollerblade. And item #1 on the Top Five List from my 100-pound-weight-loss blog seems to have weathered the test of time: "Build momentum. Slow and steady wins the race. Start slow. You'll be surprised at how quickly your momentum will build." I did just that. I started slow and haven't looked back since. Oh, and guess what? Item #2 was bang on as well: "Enjoy what you do. It should be fun and not hard." I continue to make it easy on myself and have fun. I'll leave the no-pain-no-gain approach to someone else.

May 2013. EAT Healthier. Remember, Healthier Doesn't Have to Taste Like S**t.

Eat less? That was part of the strategy. Not better at first, but at least less. As I mentioned in my 100-pound-weight-loss blog, I started eating three chocolate bars instead of four with my glass of milk before bed. Then from three to two. Before I knew it, I was down to none. I cut down on meal portions as well. A bit at a time. Next, I started to eat vegetables, and they actually tasted quite good. So, I ate more. As I note in my healthier-eating blog, "Eating healthy doesn't have to taste like S**t" became my new credo. And, eating healthy can actually taste good!

It took me a while, but I eventually changed my eating habits. That change included eating things like kefir and chia seeds. What is kefir, you ask? What are chia seeds? Good questions. I had no clue in those days. I do now. I eat them almost every day now for breakfast and guess what? They taste good and they're healthy! In the old days, I didn't eat breakfast. But one thing at a time. One step at a time. I won't repeat the Top Five List from my nutrition blog[21] here (it's on my website for your reading pleasure), but I will share the #1 item since I believe it sums up my approach quite nicely and that is –

drum roll, please – "Make it yummy (healthy but yummy)." Before I knew it, I was moving more and eating less. Eating less portion-wise and eating less s**t nutrition-wise. Another year would pass before I had built up enough momentum and changed enough bad habits into good ones before my body really started to recover, but that was enough to provide me with the energy to finally start turning things around.

Thank you, oxygen mask! And thank you, Dave, for grabbing hold of it and strapping it on. Oh and, by the way, the fact that your new healthy eating habits started to rub off on your children – bonus!

May 2015. DRINK Less (Less Booze, That Is). The Final Frontier, or So I Thought.

Drink more water and green tea is where I think Tom Rath, the author of *Eat Move Sleep*, seemed to be going with his "drink" recommendations. My focus was more on drinking less booze. I mention this in my blog and I'll mention it again here: cutting out the booze was not on my priority list in the summer of 2015. Or, so I thought, until one of my friends came up with a challenge for me.

The challenge from her went somewhat like this: give up drinking booze for 30 days, no exceptions. This was presented to me two weeks before I was to travel to Paris and London for a vacation with my son. Didn't she know these countries were associated with fine wine (the former) and a good pint of ale (the latter)? As a teetotaler, she had no idea what a sacrifice this would be! I tried to explain the rationale behind the occasional buzz, but it was lost on her. Surely the changes on the "move" and "eat" sides of my health equation were enough for one lifetime! But I found that, as I tried to explain my pro-drinking rationale to her, I started to question the logic behind it. The verbal processor in me was finally verbally-processing on this topic, and I was having trouble coming up with a whole lot of "pros." In fact, I was coming up with a list of "cons." Eventually I decided I would take a pass on the challenge. If I felt like a glass of wine or a beer every once in a while, I was going to have one, or two or three or more. We only live once, was my logic at the time. Screw the sugar. Screw the calories. I might not always be fully present with the people around me when I have my buzz on, but screw that, too. Surely, I'm allowed a couple of vices.

I did have a glass of wine in Paris and a pint of ale with my chips in London – two beers over two days, to be exact. But I haven't had a booze-buzz since that discussion in May 2015. I still enjoy a glass of wine on occasion, a maximum of two per occasion. Same for beer. That includes social and networking events; no more liquid courage when connecting with people. I just have to get by on my boyish charm.

Making the shift, or transition, from drinking a lot of booze on a regular basis to drinking a little bit of booze less often turned out to be EASYer than I'd thought. Maybe because, during that moment of reflection and as a result of the insights I gained during my poor attempt to convince my friend of the merits of being drunk, I had convinced myself that it was not something I wanted, or needed, anymore. Where there's a will, there's a way. Bye-bye, booze (at least the booze buzz) and hello, snooze. Yes, one of the benefits of not drinking to excess is that you get a better night's sleep.

Early 2016. SLEEP More. No Cheating Allowed.

I read somewhere that adults require seven to nine hours of quality sleep a night to be at their best the next day. Cheat and you pay the price. I only realized that when I stopped cheating – and, by cheating,

I mean drinking huge quantities of coffee and booze to make up for my lack of zzzz's. Well, the booze was now gone, and I was slowly replacing some of my coffee intake with decaffeinated green tea. Maybe it was time to explore the last pillar of the *Eat Move Sleep* triumvirate: Sleep. And, by sleep, I mean quality sleep, not the waking-up-every-20-minutes kind of sleep.

This lifestyle change took a while. I was skeptical at first. My doubts increased as I calculated the amount of productive time I would have to give up; time is money, and time is precious. I think now that if I had had some sort of sleep-versus-productivity baseline to inspire me, it would have made things EASYer. I didn't have one. I couldn't remember the last time I had had a long, restful sleep. Ironically, my baseline was revealed by my lack of productivity when I didn't get enough rest, rather than my increased productivity when I did.

As part of my quest to lead a more balanced lifestyle, I started to become more disciplined and aware of where I was spending my time. I started to notice that it was difficult to concentrate on the tasks at hand when I was short on sleep. Since I was now my own boss, I started a new habit. I shut down my career quadrant by leaving tasks to the next day whenever I got too tired. Guess what happened? A task that would have taken an hour to finish the day before, because I was too tired, took me 10 minutes the next morning. What an eye-opener! I guess that sleep is important after all. Time for another change, a change that involved resetting my alarm clock. Not to wake up early, but to go to bed earlier – at least until it becomes a habit.

April 2017. LOVE Yourself. Especially When You Do Eventually Cheat.

This was the month I received my latest and greatest health statistics. It had been more than two years since I had gotten back to my normal

BMI score after 15 years of hovering between overweight and obesity. My latest results? I was at my fittest ever as measured by both BMI and % of body fat. How cool! Those good habits must be taking hold after all!

As it turned out, it was also the month I cheated. I cheated by eating a bunch of cookies, not one cookie, but a bunch of cookies, over several days. Yes, I cheated, and it wasn't even what I call a "good" cheat, like joining my son for a hamburger at one of his favourite burger joints. It was what I called a "bad" cheat. It was brought on by nothing more than the desire to eat something that appealed to me when I was feeling a little bit low. Yes, those pesky emotions. So much for feeling happy all the time. So much for never cheating. It didn't happen often but, when it did, I generally felt badly about it. So much for my self-compassion.

Then, one day, I was having lunch with a friend. She had also recently undergone a healthy lifestyle change, which had resulted in a significant loss of weight. She, too, had managed to keep the weight off longer than the 90% of people who slide after a big weight loss goal is met. And, guess what? She also has times when she cheats. But unlike me, she doesn't seem to mind as much. I asked her why that was. Her answer went something like this, "I love myself. I trust myself. I know that I'll go back to my healthier ways sooner rather than later. So, I go with it. I don't get down on myself. I continue to love myself." Wow! How cool is that? I think it's about time to upgrade self-compassion to self-love. You hear that, lover boy? Time to make it EASYer on yourself by adding a little more self-love to your healthy-zone equation.

SO, WHAT DID I LEARN?

How did I make change EASYer on myself 😊 (or not ☹)?

Just lacing up the rollerblades isn't hard and skating around the block isn't far, but it doesn't get any EASYer than that. I didn't know it at the time, but that's when I first came up with what became my new modus operandi of making change EASYer on myself. It's served me well ever since, as long as I remember to keep asking myself the question each and every time I'm about to take on a new change; i.e. What can I do to make this change EASYer on myself? Oh, and it's also served me well when it comes to maintaining a change, at least until the momentum kicks in and it becomes a new habit, a positive new habit. 😊

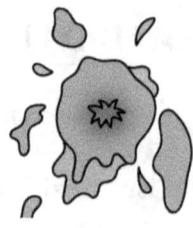

THAT WAS ALL ABOUT ME. WHAT ABOUT YOU?

What are you doing to make your journey of change EASYer on yourself? ☺ (or not ☹)?

What is your health-zone formula?

_____

_____

And, how is it working for you these days?

_____

_____

Is there one easy change you can make today in order to be healthier?

_____

_____

Chapter 15: Maintaining My Momentum

If you hear a voice within you say "you cannot paint," then by all means paint and that voice will be silenced.

Vincent van Gogh

That big black nasty looking character on the left of the picture for this chapter is my inner critic. The scaredy cat on the right was my inner coach. I ended up hiring a new one, or at least I wished that I could have, at the time.

Battling My Inner Critic

Thinking back on all of the time I used to spend in my nasty zone, there was someone who played a big role in my spending so much time in that nasty zone. I don't like to blame others for my troubles but, in this case, I'm going to cheat and play the blame game. I'm going to blame my Inner Critic.

In fact, I'm not really cheating since he (my Inner Critic) is, technically speaking, me, or at least one part of me. Although, if he truly were part of me, why was he so nasty to me in those days? And where was his counterpart, my Inner Coach? He seems to have gone AWOL and should get some of the blame for my stay in my nasty zone as well. I don't want to pick on him too much, either, though, because, in those days, my Inner Coach had someone picking on him, and that someone was my Inner Critic. It was like a battle between my Inner Critic and my Inner Coach. My Inner Coach was not winning many, if any, of the battles.

To make a few long stories short, my Inner Coach finally did gain the confidence to start speaking up for himself and, before he knew it, he was doing most of the talking. It took time and effort, and lots of trying things out but, eventually, he, more like we, were able to get there. So, in this chapter, I thought I'd share a few stories on how I started to muzzle the other guy. These stories have one common message: Just do it. Don't listen to the other guy, just do it. No one knows what the future has in store. The only way to find things out is to try them on for size. I had tried things on at earlier stages in my transformation and that approach had served me well, so I decided to continue that approach. Here are the results of standing up to my Inner Critic.

October 2012. Standing up to My Inner Critic (and Fears). Just Showing up.

It was time to face my fears, many of which I realized later were unfounded. You'll recall that I was a little on the shy side, especially around people I thought were more senior. I think that the more accurate term is "intimidated." Intimidated because I didn't see myself as being on the same playing field as the senior partners. I felt out of place. What value could little-old-me possibly offer? I had no self-confidence. And here I was, the program director of a program targeting client C-suite executives as well as the most senior partners in the firm I worked for. I was preparing to attend a meeting with a whole bunch of them. A whole bunch of senior partners and little old me. Yikes! Good thing I still had a few cigarettes left.

Well, yes, I did end up inhaling one of those cigarettes right before the session. Yes, I did feel like an imposter in the room during the cocktail session, even after having inhaled a couple of cocktails of liquid courage, but you know what? I showed up. I conquered my fears and I just showed up. Guess what? Those senior partners were not that scary after all. As a matter of fact, the most senior of them all, the one I feared meeting the most, turned out to be the most approachable. He even invited me to sit next to him at his table during dinner and seemed to enjoy introducing me to as many people as possible.

And the more people (partners) I met, the more I found that were as approachable as that senior partner. Best of all, they were interested in what I had to say. "Hey, Dave, what did you say were the Top 10 Challenges facing CFOs in your survey? Interesting stuff! Tell me more." Wow, I actually had interesting things to share. Talk about a confidence boost! What a great bunch of leaders! I probably should have connected earlier, and without the help of a cigarette and cocktail. You hear that, Inner Coach?! I should have started listening to you earlier when you suggested I just do it. Although, I must say, you could have spoken up more often and in a louder voice. My Inner Critic can be quite loud at times.

November 2013. Standing up to My Inner Critic (and Fears). Just Standing up.

This is weird. I'm going to be on stage in front of 40 Chief Financial Officers (CFOs) in a couple of minutes and I'm not nervous. Not at all. I am co-presenting, with one of the partners, on the top priorities of the CFO, and she's insisting I take the lead in the session because I'm more familiar with the priorities we identified through our survey. Inner Critic, where are you? I can't hear you! Isn't this when you tell me that I shouldn't be up here. I'm going to screw up! I'm not a CFO! I'm not a partner! I don't know what I'm talking about. I won't know the answers to questions from the audience! Where are you, Inner Critic? Where are you hiding? Are you setting up an ambush? I'm not nervous at all. I feel so confident, and yet I'm about to go on stage any minute now!

Well, that minute passed, and I went up on that stage and things went off without a hitch. Not only did no one call me out on any of my statements, I had CFOs coming up to me after the session and during the lunch wanting to know more. These were senior level CFOs, and this was little old me. Turns out that my Inner Coach was right when he told me to just get up there and do my best. He reminded me that no one has all the answers. He reminded me that I was most likely the only one in the room who was as familiar with the CFO challenges outlined in the survey, having lived and breathed them as part of the program for the previous year. He suggested that the CFOs might be interested in knowing what challenges their fellow CFOs were facing. My Inner Coach reminded me that, if there was something I didn't know, it would be an opportunity to learn. That's how we grow. If we're unfamiliar with something, we learn about it and learning gives us the confidence to explore other areas and ask more questions. The more we learn, the more we grow; the more we grow, the more confident we become. All you have to do is just do it. Just get out there and do it, or in this case, just get up there and stand on that stage.

April 2015. Standing up to My Inner Critic (and Fears). Tackling the "S" Word.

Talking to partners and CFOs about the challenges of the role of the CFO was one thing; talking sales was quite another. Yes, sales, my dreaded "S" word. But I discovered a link between the "S" word and the relationship-building program I was becoming so passionate about. It took me a while to figure it out, but figure it out I did. My program made the connection. It was about developing trusted relationships with CFOs in order to increase the sales the firm did with them and their organizations. The theory was that trusted relationships ultimately lead to sales.

And what better way to start developing trust than to engage in discussions on the top priorities and challenges of the CFO? Okay, I get it now. That's why we created the CFO survey – in order to understand CFO challenges and priorities better. Interesting. Relationships lead to sales. So, selling is really about developing relationships! Cool. That sure involved a mind shift or, in this case, a word shift. Replace the word "sales" with "relationship-building!" I'm really getting into the developing-relationships concept these days, a little late in the game, but I'm catching up quickly.

I had the chance to catch up even quicker when I was contacted to see if I would be interested in helping to develop and deliver a national webinar on sales. I was the only non-partner invited to participate. At first, I was confused, "Why me? I'm not a partner!" I was flattered. I was a bit sceptical about whether or not I could pull it off, but that's when my Inner Coach showed up and told me to just do it. So, I did. I tested it out on a group of peers. I asked for feedback. And in the end, I just did it. And guess what? It was one of the most watched learning webinars of its kind at the firm, with more than 600 people tuning in to watch. Gee, thanks for the push, Inner Coach! Take that, Inner Critic!

May 2015. Standing up to My Inner Critic (and Fears). Just Speaking up.

Although I was making progress in tuning out my Inner Critic and focusing more on my Inner Coach, my Inner Critic was not ready to give up. He was not going away without a fight. As I would later learn, he will likely never give up and go away, so I had to manage him accordingly, but that is a story for later. For now, back to the battle that took place during another sales webinar. This time, I wasn't leading it, I was just listening in.

It was a webinar whose potential audience was the 9,000-plus partners and employees within the Canadian firm, including my colleagues and peers from across Canada. The webinar was being led by a partner who was one of my heroes on both the sales and leadership fronts. What a treat! It was about using storytelling to sell. Although I was just starting to get comfortable with the "S" word, I really liked storytelling, both telling and hearing stories. And here was one of my heroes telling a story and then answering questions on it during the question period at the end of the presentation. And guess what? I had a question. The question was not the important part of this story. What was important was that I was afraid to ask it.

I was still revelling in the success of the recent webinar I had led, but here I was, a short time later, afraid to even ask a simple question.

My Inner Critic was back with a vengeance. "Don't ask that question, it's stupid," he warned. "Your hero is leading the call. He'll think you're an idiot. The rest of the learning team will think you're a loser and that will mean no more webinars for you! Everyone on the call will think you don't know what you're talking about. You're an idiot. You're a loser." Should I bite my tongue and not ask the question? But before I could start biting, my Inner Coach swooped in. "Dave, just do it. Just ask. Trust me! Trust yourself," my Inner Coach countered, encouraging me to pay no attention to my Inner Critic. There was some back and forth but, eventually, I did it. I trusted my Inner Coach and I sent in my question. By the time I had found the nerve to send it, there was only time for one more – and a whole bunch were sent in at the same time. Mine was selected. Before my hero responded, with some great insights I might add, he first mentioned what a great question it was. And, to think I almost didn't send it in!

And what was the question? It was, "Do we learn more from hearing success stories or horror stories?" The response: "Everyone is unique and different. Some prefer both. Some prefer one over the other." And that's why, in the case of my book and my blogs, I include both. The good, the bad, the just plain ugly and the great. What can I say? I'm a big fan of inclusivity when it comes to storytelling.

July to November 2015. Standing up to My Inner Critic (and Fears). Just Plain Having Fun.

Presentations to CFOs and partners. Design and delivery of webinars on relationship-selling. What challenge was next for the newly emerging Captain Courageous? The next one also had to do with the "S" word. The firm was putting together a relationship-selling professional development offering and I was asked if I would like to be one of the facilitators. I was the only one asked who did not have a sales role and background. It sounded like fun. After an initial conversation with my Inner Coach, I accepted the offer. And guess what? It was fun. Over the next six months, I led or co-led more than a dozen sessions with several hundred partners and practitioners in the firm. I enjoyed each and every one. The days of hiding under a table at the mere mention of the "S" word seemed to be over.

Before I knew it, I had a new habit. I was starting to believe in myself. And that belief started to give me something else I hadn't felt in a while, and that was courage. The courage to try a whole bunch of things. And guess what? I actually liked a lot of them, even ones with the "S" word. Thank you, Inner Coach. Thanks for nothing, Inner Critic.

SO, WHAT DID I LEARN?

How did I make change EASYer on myself ☺ (or not ☹)?

Sometimes when I think of my Inner Coach and my Inner Critic(s) (or gremlins, as I sometimes like to call them), I picture a seesaw. On one side, the one with the coach on it, there is the word Positivity and on the other side, the one with the critics and/or gremlins, there is the word Negativity. I want to keep the side of the seesaw that provides me with the positivity (i.e. positive energy) as high in the air as possible. EASYer said than done when I have all of these other nasty characters (i.e. my Inner Critics and gremlins) constantly trying to pull me and the seesaw down to their side, the one with the negative mindset.

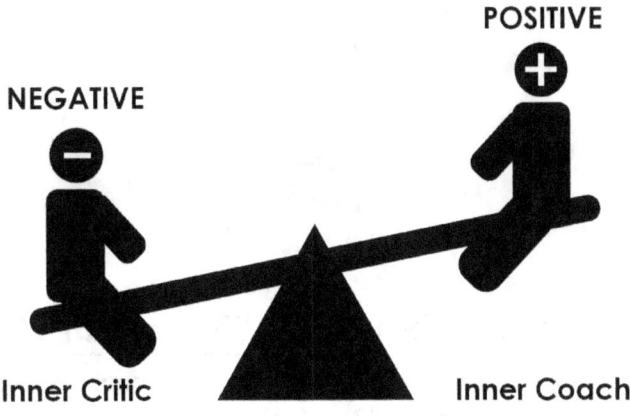

How have I made it EASYer for my Inner Coach, and me, to keep that seesaw slanted in the right direction? One concept that comes to mind is the "Power of Positivity" and maintaining a positive mindset. I know, EASYer said than done. It can get pretty scary when those scary times come around and, unless you've decided to stay in your comfort zone, rest assured, they will come around ☹. When they do come, it certainly doesn't hurt to have worked with your Inner Coach, and others, on building a little self-confidence, or a lot ☺. The self-confidence that is gained by moving forward and trying things on for size. As Henry Ford put it, "Whether you think you can or whether you think you can't, you're right."

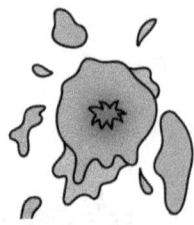

That was all about me. What about YOU?
What are you doing to make your journey of change EASYer on yourself? 😊 (or not ☹)?

Are there particular situations where your Gremlins show up?

_____

_____

Who is winning your battle with your inner critic(s) and/or gremlins?

_____

Where is your confidence level?

_____

What kinds of activities will enhance your confidence?

_____

_____

Chapter 16: Finding My Calling

*People rarely succeed unless
they have fun in what they are doing.*

Dale Carnegie

My objective, at this point in my career search time, was to come up with a Top Five List: a one-pager of what I was looking for in my career. It took me six months to come up with that list. I cheated a bit. I couldn't narrow them down to a Top Five, so I settled for a Top Seven. Oh well, could be worse and I am a big James Bond fan ☺ Agent 007. It was this list, that I am about to share on the next page that ended up really shaping my calling, and calling me out of my comfort zone. Big time!

MY Career Criteria Top ~~5~~ 7 List
I am seeking a Career that provides me with the following ...

1. **Autonomy (a.k.a. Choice)**: I call the shots. Input welcome but final call on "priorities" and "path" rests with me.

2. **Flexibility:** I don't want to miss out on any opportunities so want to be able to turn on a dime.

3. **Work life balance:** I have other passions to explore as well so I can't afford to be out of balance on career side.

4. **Doing what I love (a.k.a. nurturing my core)**: I love the feeling of being energized and passionate about what I do.

5. **Making an impact**: I have this burning "desire" to try and help "make others better off". An opportunity to share my own personal "ongoing transformation" which I believe could help inspire others in right circumstances.

6. **Master of my domain(s)**: I like the feeling of being the one people turn to for support and guidance. An opportunity for on-going personal and professional development is essential so I can stay current on key topics.

7. **Opportunity to develop a broad and diverse network**: I get my energy and ideas from others. Working with inspiring peers and colleagues and clients is very important. The more the merrier, from far and wide.

March 2015. Developing My Revised Approach to Career Transitions. Pulling a "Costanza"!

Finding my calling? Searching for my calling would be a more accurate description of what I was up to back then. The timing was perfect, though. I was coming up on the five-year mark in my role. I was coming up on the big 2-0 (20 years of employment) at the firm and I had just hit the big 5-0 of my life on planet Earth. A bit of a triple whammy! Although I was still enjoying my time at the firm and thoughts of working anywhere else seemed remote, almost incomprehensible back then, my program was winding down and I was looking for a change of scenery. The big question had become, what is my next move, i.e. role?

It was time to explore a career change again. It could be argued that I hadn't done a whole lot of exploring the last time. The falling-on-my-sword approach to career change almost five years earlier was probably not aligned with best practices. It was all that I could think of at the time, so I'm not going to beat myself up over it. This time around, however, I wanted to try a different approach. The approach I chose was as different as it could get.

I decided to do the opposite of what I had done last time. I decided to follow the same approach that served George Costanza so well in one of my favourite *Seinfeld* episodes; the episode in which George decided to do the opposite of what he usually did. One of those opposite approaches was being *authentic*. It doesn't get any more authentic than the way that George introduced himself to a woman he was interested in at the local deli. His approach went something like this: "Hello, my name is George. I'm unemployed and I live with my parents." (I'll leave it to you to Google that episode if you'd like to know how things turned out for George.) George's two tricks – doing the opposite and being authentic – are what I tried as I explored my next career move. And, in honour of George, I would name my new doing-the-opposite approach "Pulling a Costanza".

So, what was the opposite of what I had done the last time I had questioned my career? If I were to summarize it in one word, that word would be connecting. I had connected with no one the last time around. This time, I was going to connect with a whole bunch of folks. I was going to connect with them with one purpose in mind. A win-win role within the firm was the goal. In the end, I would reach out to more than 20 partners in the firm, many of them in some of the most senior leadership positions, including almost half of the direct reports of the CEO. Yes, little old me, non-partner me, reached out to all of these senior partners and asked for 15 minutes of their time. What's the worst thing they could do? Say no? Not answer my email? It was just an email. Go ahead, Dave, my Inner Coach implored, just give it a try! So, I did.

I reached out to everyone on my list and they all accepted, and many even commented positively on my proactive approach. Cool. I probably should have started being more proactive a long time ago. This Costanza approach works. Do the opposite. In this case, be proactive, not reactive. Noted for future reference.

Before connecting with all these folks, there was one other person I hadn't connected with previously, and that one person was little old me. In discussing win-win scenarios, it might come in handy if I had known more about what I was looking for. Such had not been the case the previous time. Not only did I have no ideas of what a WIN was for me when I had decided to fall on my sword, I had no clue how to come up with any. It was time to pull another Costanza. In this case, I would come up with a list of criteria that I could use to evaluate the various opportunities available to me. This was probably not a bad way to get to know myself a little better at the same time. Double whammy! Awesome!

October 31, 2015. The Big Day. The Big Deadline. Do I Stay? Or Do I Go?

As I started to develop my career criteria list, I realized that the exercise was more difficult than I had anticipated. My objective was to come up with the Top Five criteria for my dream job, and I was somewhere north of 60 of them. The longer I worked on the list, the more I added. I also found that the more I connected and discussed opportunities with others, the more questions I came away with to ponder, which often meant revisiting the list. Hey, this expanding-one's-lens concept was making things more complicated! Expanding my lens was expanding my list! I had better give myself a deadline or this could drag on forever. Let's see now, I love Halloween. How about Halloween as a deadline? That should be enough time. All righty, then. Pitter patter, let's get at 'er. Let's get at that list and get it down to my Top Five.

I didn't get my list down to a Top Five, I had to settle for a Top Seven, which was the mid-point between a David Letterman Top 10 list and a David Walker Top Five blog list. Nor did it take until October 31 to answer the question. I came up with the answer a week before my self-imposed deadline. It wasn't the answer I was expecting.

Based on the criteria I had developed and my discussions with partners and many others (including a career coach assigned to me by the firm), my next career move was going to be one I hadn't considered when I had set out. My next transition was going to be a transition, not only in role, not only in organization, but a transition right out of my Career-related Life Quadrant completely. After more than 30 years of working in my Career Quadrant, I was going to transition into what I now refer to as my Business Quadrant, and it was going to be my business. I was going to be working for a new boss, me.

Talk about a transition! I was transitioning out of one of my Life Quadrants completely. A transition from a Career Quadrant (which included bi-weekly paycheques, an employer-sponsored pension plan, an employer-sponsored and maintained business infrastructure and tools, etc.) to a Business Quadrant (which would have to eventually include not only a business infrastructure and services, but also clients willing to pay to fund my business and life expenses), and that meant, yes, the "S" word, "sales."

And this from the guy who was fast approaching the age at which he was hoping to never work another day in his life. This from the guy who, until about a year earlier, was scared s**tless of the word "sales." Now for some reason, he was no longer scared, despite never having sold a thing in his life. This was a guy who had recently become a single parent with two young children to provide for. What had happened to Captain Comfort Zone? This was a pretty radical shift. What gives? There were a lot of "what gives"-type questions back then, two of which resonated with me the most. One related to something I did; the other related to something someone said (more about that shortly). What I did was take care of myself.

I had taken care of myself by taking better care of my self-confidence through my efforts over the previous few years on the job front, and I had taken better care of myself by taking care of my health. I had taken care of neither, previously, and my energy level during those times reflected that neglect. Now, thanks to my revised approach, my energy levels were right up there. Talk about pulling a Costanza! The difference in my approach to my health and my career over the previous few years can only be described as night and day. I had done the opposite of what had gotten me to that nasty place the last time around. I had pulled a Costanza.

Now, back to what that someone said. That someone was one of the partners I had connected with as part of my connecting-with-people strategy. I can't remember the exact conversation, but it went something like this, "Dave, you make people better off. It's part of your DNA. You might want to consider ways in which you can do more of that, including exploring coaching. If you end up doing so within the firm, great; if not, then it's the firm's loss, and the world's gain." Wow. Talk about a morale booster! This was quite an eye-opener and a boost to my self-esteem! Although I didn't realize the implications at the time, and I wasn't sure I believed what he was sharing with me, that chat and those comments were life-and career-altering moments. There was a lot more to learn about myself by talking to others! So much for my isolationist approach of the past. What had I been thinking?

I continued to connect with others and, as I did, I started to shape my career-choice criteria. More importantly, I started to get to know myself better. Before I knew it, I answered that all-important question – one week before I had committed to doing so: Do I stay, or do I go? It was time to go. It was time to go and help some people help themselves to become better off. After all, that was supposedly in my DNA. Thanks for that feedback, Jeff. And, thanks to all the many others who took the time out of their extremely busy schedules to help me. To help make not only me better off, but potentially many others better off as well…my clients and, as it would eventually turn out, my readers.

November 30, 2015. Taking the Plunge.

You don't know what you don't know. Have you heard that before? Well, that was the pickle I was in. I was pretty close to taking the plunge, but I was still struggling with my choices of potential service offerings. Life coaching? Professional speaking? Writing stuff that people would pay for? Group coaching? Facilitation? I had experience facilitating. I had done some coaching, but not any life coaching. And I had never run my own (or anyone else's) business before. What was I thinking? Was this really the right thing to do? That's when my career coach made a comment that, let's just say, sealed the deal. My career coach reminded me that, until I actually tried, how could I possibly know if I'd like it? How could I possibly know if it would work? Just give it a try. I had some savings. I could always find something else to do later, if things didn't work out.

All righty, then. Let's do it. Let's give it a try. I pulled the trigger. On November 30, 2015, Captain Comfort Zone returned his laptop to his employer. It was okay, because Captain Courageous had already picked up a new one. A new one for a new business, for my new business. Oh, and Captain Courageous also picked up the tab for a new cell phone; it turned out that my old one belonged to my now-ex-employer as well.

SO, WHAT DID I LEARN?

How did I make change EASYer on myself 😊 (or not ☹)?

Getting to know myself (my "WHO") better, i.e. getting a better handle on MY values and MY needs and MY wants enabled me to align more closely with them! That's how I would summarize this chapter of my mid-life transition. I hadn't spent a whole lot of time on that all-important exercise in the past, so when it came time to catching up, it took me a while. It took me a while to connect with a lot of other people, and it took me a while to connect with myself. I had ignored that type of information and those connections in the past, and, in hindsight, it hadn't served me well. ☹

But now that I had decided to pull a Costanza, I couldn't ignore others – and especially not myself – any longer. Did I completely catch up on getting to know myself better during this phase of my self-transformation? I thought I had, but the catching up had just started. Getting to know myself better (my unique WHO), and what makes me tick, was going to continue, at an even faster pace, as part of my upcoming adventure. My career decision was made. And, I can't tell you how much having well-vetted decision criteria – and a timeframe within which to make that decision – made it EASYer on me to make that decision, especially one of such importance to me and my loved ones. Thanks for the inspiration, George. 😊

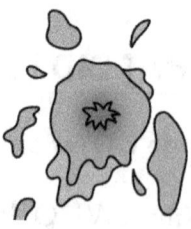

That was all about me. What about YOU?

What are you doing to make your journey of change EASYer on yourself? ☺ (or not ☹)?

Are you exploring a potential career transition in your near future?

_____

What is life going to be like if you don't make a change?

_____

_____

What could life be like if you did make a change?

_____

_____

Would it be a good idea to review and update your decision-making criteria?

_____

_____

Can you give yourself a deadline for enhancing that list?

_____

_____

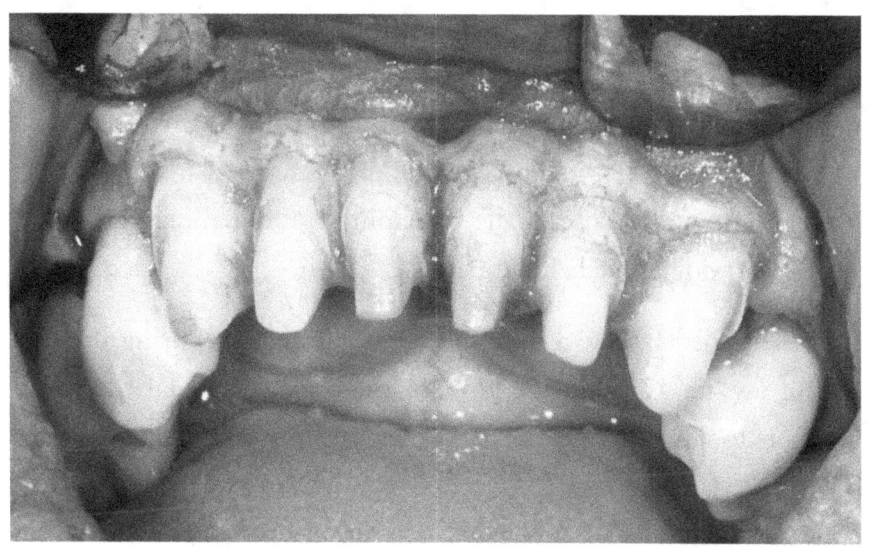

Chapter 17: Firming up My Foundation

To love oneself is the beginning of a life-long romance.

Oscar Wilde

A picture of my teeth, or what was left of them, six hours into 34 hours' worth of dental surgery over the course of a little more than a year. It cost me the equivalent of my first year's salary in the workforce.

Note to self: Remember the principle of compound interest. It applies not only to money, but also to maintaining your body. Or, in this case, not maintaining it. The cost and price of neglect compounds quickly.

April 2014 to March 2016. Flossing My Teeth. First, I Need Some Teeth to Floss.

In a few minutes, you're going to read about a 100-point self-assessment that I took in early 2016. For one item, I scored one point if I brushed my teeth daily. I was eventually able to make that one a habit and check that one off my list. It had not been much of a habit previously and the result was that I no longer had many teeth left. I had neglected my teeth and the rest of my body for so long that I was losing teeth and the use of the remaining teeth at an alarming rate, yet I wasn't doing much about it.

I had stopped taking care of myself at some point during the first half of my life. I couldn't be bothered with regular dental check-ups (or visits to any other heath care professionals, for that matter). Sure, if I had a cavity I would have it filled, but that was exceptional. I don't even think I had any dental floss in my apartment when I was younger, and I certainly didn't use it if I did. When my teeth started to crack, and I started to lose teeth on the right side of my mouth, I started eating on the left side. That was my approach in those days. My mom would not have been proud. It never occurred to me to find out what was causing my teeth to crack. I finally got around to it after I had decided to take better care of myself, only to discover that my mouth was out of alignment, which caused my teeth to grind together at night. They were grinding and slowly disappearing, knocking my "Colgate smile" into oblivion along the way. I had neglected myself and my health and it had taken its toll. Kind of like the concept of compound interest in accounting but, in this case, it was the result of neglecting my body that was compounding and not the money. Luckily for me, I had some money that was compounding. It was my Freedom 55 retirement plan. So, when I finally decided to focus, and invest in living a healthier and happier life – rather than hoping for the fantasy concept of eventual freedom and happiness that a corporate marketing campaign had flashed before my eyes – I had the cash available to fix myself.

When I finally decided to start taking care of myself (and my teeth), I spent more than 30 hours in the dentist's chair in a little more than a year. One session alone lasted more than six hours, the time it takes me to drive from Montreal to see my family in Toronto. When my kids complain about the length of that car ride, I ask them if they'd prefer to be in the dentist's chair instead. And guess what? There's just so much freezing that can safely be administered in one session. I found that out the hard way. It was toward the end of my six-hour session when the dental surgeon was suturing my gums. The freezing was wearing off. He was not quite done but it was too dangerous to give me any more. "Tough it out, Dave. I know you're an accountant and not a superhero, but tough it out. I'm almost done." Yikes! Thirty plus hours in the chair. And that was just the time involved. Think of the cost. All of those hours in the dentist's chair could have been used coaching clients, creating clients, writing stories, sharing stories, etc. In accounting jargon, we call that cost the "opportunity cost." And what about the cost of the procedure itself? Let's put it this way. It was the same amount of money I made in my first year out of university. Remind me not to let things slip again.

When the dental work was finally finished, it took me a while to get used to chewing food on both sides of my mouth, but I must say I like it! Oh, and looking in the mirror and admiring my "new" Colgate smile? It's priceless!

March 25, 2016. I Got My Test Results. My Personal Foundation Test Results. Time for a Sabbatical.

One of the first courses I took as I embarked upon my new journey as a professional coach and business owner was called "personal foundations." Apparently, it was important that, if we coaches were going to coach others properly, we had to have our own house in order. Okay, that made sense, but how was I supposed to measure whether my personal foundation was solid? My coaching school came up with a 100-point self-assessment program called the "Clean Sweep."[22] Okay, then, bring it on!

I had spent the previous few years working on firming up my personal foundation on the personal and professional sides of things, so this should be a walk in the park. Maybe I could get an exemption from this course? That was my initial thinking, until I actually took the self-assessment and came out with a score of 56 out of 100. What was with that? I had barely passed!

There were four sections to the assessment:

1. Physical Environment

2. Health and Emotional Balance

3. Money

4. Relationships

I scored low on all of the questions, with the exception of the ones that were related to my health. I was not surprised to score low on the money side of things, given my annual revenues had fallen to zero dollars the day I handed my computer in to my former employer, but my relationship scores were even lower. Yikes! It might be time to consider some type of Relationship 101 course. While I was at it, I might also need an Emotional Intelligence 101 course. My scores in that category were nothing to write home about, either.

My own coach informed me that my score was actually not that bad for someone who was just starting out in coaching, but I'm not sure that resonated with me. After all, I was the guy who had just pulled a 180 on the healthy living front. I had just lost 100 pounds of body fat. I was the guy who had summoned up the courage to make one of the boldest career transitions in, well, in his career. All of that to end up with a score of 56. How could that be? It looked like I had more work ahead of me than I had thought.

"Okay, Mr. Taking-it-EASYer-on-yourself, how are you going to pull this one off?" I asked myself. "Starting up a new business, your first, AND firming up your personal foundation, which apparently needs a fair bit of firming up, especially on the relationship and emotional fronts. And then there's that "F" word, Finances." Hmmm. Good question.

Well, I came up with what I thought was a good answer. It took me a couple of months to figure this little trick out, but eventually I did. My answer (idea) was to take a year off. I would take a one-year sabbatical but, rather than backpack around the world or search for meaning on remote mountaintops, I would focus 50% of my sabbatical on firming up my personal foundation and 50% on launching my business. I had yet to take a sabbatical in my 50 plus years of life and what better topics to explore than these two?

So, I did it. How did that change my approach you might ask? There was not much difference on the activity side of my ledger, but the sabbatical made a huge difference on the stress side, since I no longer had revenue targets. I didn't have targets because I was on sabbatical; as such, I didn't feel as if I had a gun to my head forcing me to meet revenue targets, short- or long-term. I was free to pursue my life at a comfortable pace. I could connect with whomever I wanted. I could explore whatever I wanted. No pressure. In the interim, I would fund my business with savings. There was no rush. There was no urgency.

I had worked hard during the first half of my life and it was now time to enjoy myself. It was time to enjoy developing myself further personally and professionally. It was time to enjoy my sabbatical! A sabbatical within my half-time journey of transformation.

August 2016. Tackling the "L" Word.

Summer of 2016. It was time to take on the relationship section of my dismal self-assessment score. Not only had I neglected my teeth during the latter stages of the first half of my life, but I had neglected a lot of relationships. I was getting better, but I was far from where I wanted to be. So, I decided to take a page from David Letterman and use his "Top 10 List" approach to tackle this objective. I would put together a list of the Top 10 relationships I would like to strengthen. Then I would come up with an approach that would allow me to connect with each person on the list and score points in the relationship section. As a bonus, this would push me out of my comfort zone.

It didn't take long to figure out a way to do all of the above. I was going to go for broke. I would use the one word that caused me more angst than the dreaded "S" word and that was the "L" word, Love. As I reviewed the questions, it dawned on me that I couldn't remember the last time I had told someone, with the exception of my children, that I loved them. It had been so long that I had trouble saying it. Just imagining myself saying those words stressed me out. Guys are not supposed to be saying words like that. We like to talk about sports and work and other guy-things, not love.

Okay, that's what I would do. I would tell some folks that I loved them. Not just anyone, but people who I actually loved. I would start with a sub-set of the names on my list; in this case, my father, my brother and my sister. I would tell them that I loved them. That should get me a few more points on the self-assessment. Well, it was EASYer said than done. After all, this was the "L" word and I was the shy, ostrich guy. How was I going to make this one EASYer on myself?

Ultimately, I decided to practise with a friend of mine, a friend I had worked with for a long time. We had become not just colleagues, but very good friends during our time together. I like to share with her. She's a great listener and seems to understand this stuff. I'm a dude, a Martian; she, thankfully, is not. I could practise with her, then try it out on my sister. It might be EASYer to start with my friend, given our long-standing relationship.

So, I set up a call with my friend, and I practised my pitch. I was ready to sign off from the call with my friend and try it out for real on my sister. I was working up to it when my friend told me something. She told me she loved me. I immediately responded that I loved her, too. Gee, could it be that easy? Then I called my sister and told her that I loved her, she replied, "Thanks for sharing that with me, Dave. I know that. You didn't have to tell me. I already knew it, but thanks for saying it. How cute." On my sister's next visit with her daughters, the first thing they all said as they got out of the car was "we love you." And my response? Yes, the dreaded "L" word. I love you, too. It is easy. It is! Or more like, it can be.

SO, WHAT DID I LEARN?

How did I make change EASYer on myself ☺ (or not ☹)?

Have you ever heard of the concept that "it all starts with YOU"? Making and maintaining a change starts and stops with YOU! If that's the case, and you're the one who makes it all happen, doesn't it make sense that taking care of yourself will help you make that change a lot EASYer on yourself?

I'm not sure if it was EASYer neglecting myself in the first place ☹ or putting myself back together again like Humpty Dumpty. Talk about a lack of self-maintenance! And a lack of self-care. A lack of self-love. And it wasn't just my teeth. When I finally decided to turn things around, I spent a lot of time with a whole lot of other health professionals, including some I'd never heard of before. I underwent quite the transformation. If you want photographic proof, I've included enough pictures in this book to hopefully get that point across. There are plenty more on my website (www.davewcoachingandstorytelling.com), if you require more evidence. It was my choice to let myself fall apart, and it was my choice to put myself back together. Sure, it was costly, but you know what? I'm worth it. Self-care and self-love, welcome back! I LOVE YOU, buddy! Oh, and Dad and Val and Rob, I LOVE the three of YOU as well! ☺

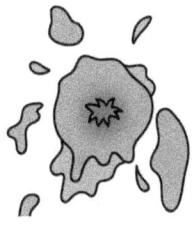

That was all about me. What about YOU?

What are you doing to make your journey of change EASYer on yourself? ☺ (or not ☹)?

What have you been neglecting?

_____

_____

How much is that neglect costing you?

_____

_____

What will the compounded cost of that neglect be in another three years? Five years?

_____

_____

What's one thing you can do right now to stop neglecting that/those issue(s)?

_____

_____

Chapter 18: Finding the Authentic Me

Be who you are and say what you feel, because those who mind don't matter and those who matter don't mind.

Dr. Seuss

When it comes to making and maintaining change, they say that self-awareness is nine-tenths of the journey. And, when it comes to successfully undertaking those journeys of change, a better understanding of our WHO (what makes each of us tick) is key to choosing the best path forward (the WHAT we do and HOW we go about doing it). Hence, my focus and fascination with being more aware of my WHO. If you don't believe me, just ask to take a peek at my workbook, my "WHO are YOU" workbook!

January 2016 to August 2017: My Journey of Self-Discovery. Filling in the Sections of My "WHO Are YOU" Workbook.

My "Who are YOU," in my case, ME (a.k.a. David Arthur Walker) workbook did not start out as a workbook, but that's where it ended up – as I outline in my blog, "WHO are YOU? The Unique YOU! The Authentic YOU! How well Do YOU know YOU? Sharing MY Top 10 Ways that I got to know ME better."[23] (Boy, that's a mouthful.) There are 11 sections of self-assessments and feedback from others in my workbook. I've had to include a table of contents in it in order to keep track of them all (refer to the resources section at the end of this book for the list.) From playing to my strengths, to reaching for my dreams, to not being shy to share my love language. I've covered a lot of topics on my journey of self-discovery and self-awareness over the past couple years. I've taken a lot of self-assessments during that time and I mean a lot. I like to joke that, if I had a nickel for every self-assessment I've taken, I would be a millionaire and being a millionaire would add a few points in the financial section of my self-assessment score.

All joking aside, although gaining a better understanding of myself hasn't made me rich, I'm better off in many other ways. And that's a good thing. I've come to the realization that my journey of self-discovery will continue for the rest of my life as I continue to change with changing times and situations and people who are part of that life. But this journey of self-discovery, and all the self-assessments and time spent reflecting and discussing the results of them with others, started out with a simple personality test. Until I was called out by one of my program leaders at my former employer, I believed I was someone I was not. My true personality was almost the polar opposite of what I had thought it was at that time. Not only did I not feel comfortable in my own skin, I didn't even know what my own skin was!

Not having a good handle on my own preferences and communication style at the time affected not only the way I interacted with others, but also the way in which I interacted with myself, and the type of activities in which I invested my time. This was a real eye-opener! It was an "Ah-ha moment," as we call them in coaching. And the timing was great. This occurred about a year before I was to decide to revisit my current role and employer. I can't tell you how much EASYer that exercise became after having gained a better sense of what made me tick.

I became such a believer in the power of understanding my preferences and communication styles better (as well as those of other people I interact with) that I actually obtained my accreditation on one of the tools I had used and started developing and delivering sessions on the concept. Ironically, connecting with others turned out to be a significant part of my personality, one which I only really realized when I finally decided to connect with myself. This all started with, you guessed it, a self-assessment. Self-discovery and self-assessments. Bring them on! And don't forget feedback from others. The right kind of feedback from the right kind of others. People telling you what you should do based on what they think you should do and/or what they would or have done is not what I would qualify as the right type of feedback. But feedback from people who understand your personality type and how that affects your preferences in life...worth its weight in gold!

February 2016. Finding MY GPS. It Ended Up Taking Me a Year.

Now that I had discovered, or maybe re-discovered, my personality and my preferences, I was ready to tackle more dimensions of myself, and my foundational coaching courses provided the perfect opportunity to do so. I still remember one of my first classes, when we discussed the importance of one's unique and authentic values. They were described as being our GPS. Our GPS (set of values) helps guide us on our respective unique life journeys by keeping us on the straight and narrow or, at the very least, by letting us know when we venture off in the wrong direction. This sounded good to me. Was there a self-assessment I could use to find out what mine were? Turned out there were many. Just Google it, and you'll find hundreds, if not thousands, to choose from. I know. I did it. I tried a few. Some resonated and some did not. In the end, I made a few of my own tools to help me.

I love movies. So, I developed a system of associating myself with characters in scenes from some of my favourite movies. Take the scene from a James Bond movie, starring Daniel Craig, where toward the end of the movie he lets down his armour and expresses his feelings to the character played by Eva Green. To me, this was an example of a pretty tough guy sharing his emotions, which in turn helped me feel a bit more comfortable in sharing mine, even though I was a guy. Not a tough guy like James Bond, but a guy nonetheless. Another example is Steve Martin's father character in *Parenthood*. His devotion to his children reminds me so much of how important my children are to me. If I were to apply this approach to a television series, I would identify with Phil Dunphy, from *Modern Family*, as a father figure. Talk about someone who likes to have a lot of fun and spending time with his kids!

I came up with another approach to getting traction on what was important to me as well and, if you guessed that it involved a Top 10 List, you guessed right. I wanted to come up with my Top 10 Values. I had done a similar exercise in the past, but I found that there weren't enough values to choose from, so I reached out to my fellow coaches and I came up with a list of 500, which soon became 502. It took a while but as I reflected on them and shared them with others who knew me, I was able to reduce that list to a Top 100, then a Top 25 and, finally, a Top 10. It took me about a year to finally firm up my list but, remember, I was discovering and changing a lot during that period. Good thing I had decided to build my tool in Excel. It's EASYer to change and update than Word is.

This was a time that involved a lot of self-reflection and connecting with others. So much for the quick tool kit and six weeks of accompanying self-help webinars that are widely advertised in the self-help field. And I still had a whole set of tools and concepts to explore, including my boundaries, my needs, my leadership style... there was still more work to do on myself. Whoever said it takes time and effort to make and maintain change seems to know what they're talking about. At least I'm having fun while doing it.

And guess which values came in as my Top Two (from a list of 502)? Drum roll, please! FAMILY came in as Value #1. And, Value #2? It turns out it was learning and growth. Growth! And that from someone who was so scared to come out of his comfort zone not that long ago that he had stopped growing. More like stopped living! No wonder I was in such a dark place back in those nasty days. In hindsight, it would appear that Captain Comfort Zone was not adding a whole lot of value to my life. I'm optimistic that Captain Courageous will. And if he can't, I can always call on James Bond.

March 13, 2016. Who Are YOU? Remember to Expand Your Lens and Validate It.

As I shared earlier in my story, it was one of the partners at my previous employer who first helped me connect with the side of me that likes connecting and inspiring others. He was instrumental in helping me better understand myself or, as we refer to it in the coaching world, expand my lens on better understanding WHO I was.

I was expanding my lens and increasing my level of self-confidence at the same time as I was embarking upon a path that aligned me with my passions and preferences. And I was going somewhere I actually wanted to go. Remember, I still hadn't figured out my GPS (values) at that point, so obtaining feedback from others on how they perceived me was very helpful. It eventually helped me make the big decision to transition from employee to entrepreneur.

It wasn't until I started my own business that I really decided to reach out to others to help me, once again, to gain a better understanding of myself. This time, I was looking for feedback on something that was a bit of a new concept to me, and that was My Brand. My personal brand (WHO is that David Arthur Walker guy?). In the past, my employer and my employer's business often influenced me when it came time to coming up with my brand (e.g. "I am a consultant for one of the largest professional services firms in the world.").

Now, here I was, both employee and employer. What to do? Luckily for me, as part of my sabbatical, I had decided to enrol in a series of webinars meant to help people like me launch a business. One of the exercises was to come up with our personal brands and a little elevator pitch to go along with it. So, I got busy taking a pass at mine and, before I knew it, I had dozens to choose from, but I couldn't nail it all down to just one. I kept revisiting and revising them, tweaking them this way and that. One day I found myself in, of all places, an elevator with a former colleague, and he asked what I was up to. I totally panicked and blew it. Yikes! So much for my elevator pitch.

One of the webinars I took suggested we reach out to others for feedback on how they perceived us. This was to help us gain a better understanding of ourselves so we could more easily develop our brands and elevator pitches. I was all for it. I had nothing to lose. In the worst case, no one would reply. So, reach out I did, using a tool which was named, appropriately enough, REACH™ [24]. I reached out to my former colleagues and peers and friends. The resulting feedback, which was anonymous, seemed to back up what that partner and others had been telling me when I first decided to leave and start my own business. That sure was cool! It all helped me shape my brand and my confidence and, ultimately, my pitch. Thanks for the insights and feedback, folks!

And, what was that feedback? In this case, with this particular tool, it appeared that my "Brand Persona" seemed to bode well for the coaching and storytelling service offerings I was exploring. According to those around me, the ranking of my Top Three Brand Personas[25] were:

1. **The Evangelist**: Someone who quickly inspires those around them with their fervor.

2. **The Truth-teller**: Someone who is honest. Those around them know they can trust what they say.

3. **The Self-starter**: They have the energy and drive within themselves to make things happen.

Amazing! And, my #1 leadership competency? "Inspiring[26], which includes such attributes as activating, inspiring, nurturing, empowering and developing others." Oh! And, what did I come up with as my elevator pitch? Here it is:

"Inspiring, empowering and accompanying my clients, readers and audiences in making and maintaining positive changes in their lives by helping them make those changes EASYer on themselves!"

May 2017. MY Personality. You're an Entrepreneur, Not!

In addition to the encouragement I received from others, and from my own self-refection, there was one other item that gave me more self-confidence as I was embarking upon my transition from employee to entrepreneur. It came as a bit of a surprise to me at the time to hear from someone who claimed to be familiar with the Meyer's Briggs Type Indicator (MBTI) 16 personality-type assessment[27]. Apparently my personality type was that of an Entrepreneur. It had taken me this long to find that out! Oh well, once again, better late than never. So, off went the entrepreneur to start his new business.

I received another surprise about a year-and-a-half later. It turns out that my MBTI personality, ENTP, was not that of an entrepreneur after all. ESTP is the entrepreneur. My source had inverted a letter somehow. It turned out that I had the "Debater" personality. Oops! Supposedly entrepreneurs like "living on the edge." That was not me! My biggest fear, like that of many others, was over finances and having money to pay the rent and eat. Living on the edge did not appeal to me one bit. As far as I was concerned, the sooner I could get my business up and running, the better.

It was too late now! I'll be closing in on two years before I know it. Good thing that, from what I'm reading, not everyone has to be a true entrepreneur to start a business. I'll let you know how it goes, maybe in another book, maybe in a couple of years. After all, they say it takes about five years to set up and maintain a new business. I still have a way to go but, for now, I'm having fun. I'm also learning and growing more than I have at any other point in my life and, as I pointed out earlier, learning and growing and failing (First Attempt In Learning) is one thing I really VALUE, a LOT. How cool is that?

SO, WHAT DID I LEARN?

How did I make change EASYer on myself ☺ (or not ☹)?

Ever hear of the concept of playing to your strengths? How about taking that concept to a much broader and more powerful level by playing to your YOU (a.k.a. YOUR WHO). The real you! The authentic you! Playing to you. My hypothesis, which I've been testing on myself for the past few years, is that it's EASYer to be you, the more you get to know yourself! ☺ After all, it's hard to be authentic if you don't really know yourself. And, keep at it. Remember, the only constant is change. Your situation will change and so will the people you spend time with.

And, speaking of people we spend time with, once again, thanks to everyone who provided feedback on my "ME." I am blessed to have such a caring and supportive group of colleagues and friends. And let's not forget, thanks to me for having taken the initiative to get to know MYself better in the first place. Remember, it all starts with you, or in my case, with me.

Be yourself, everyone else is already taken.
Oscar Wilde

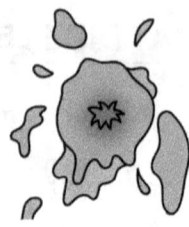

That was all about me. What about YOU?

What are you doing to make your journey of change EASYer on yourself? ☺ (or not ☹)?

WHO are you?

_____

_____

And, just as importantly, are you playing to your real and authentic you?

_____

_____

How do you know?

_____

_____

Whose lenses have you consulted?

_____

_____

Chapter 19: Finding My Mojo

*Courage is being scared to death,
but saddling up anyway.*

John Wayne

This is a picture of me on stage at my first professional-speaking gig. It took courage, not to mention a lot of practice. Courage comes from self-confidence, which often comes from practice. And, as I was about to find out, that self-confidence is also related to following through on commitments to myself. But, next time around, someone remind me NOT to commit to hauling a 100-pound barbell on stage! ☺

January 2016. Coaching 101. Oh, oh! Not again. Lost again.

In a previous chapter, I told you about the time I spent an hour with one of the partners of the program I was looking into joining as he explained the program concept to me. It went in one ear and out the other. I felt like I was in front of him again now, except that it was about five years later, and I was in my first coaching class. Yes, coaching. One of the potential service offerings I had yet to even try. Yikes! Comfort zone, where are you? Coaching is not advising. Come again? I've been advising people for the past 20 plus years and now you want me to bite my tongue when it comes to providing advice? The agenda belongs to the coachee. Are you serious? So, what am I supposed to do? My coaching style? Is that the same thing as my elevator pitch? At 50 years of age, I felt like I was back in school. Feeling lost. Learning things for the first time. Not again!

Well, you know what? Things were different now. After the initial shock wore off, I realized that I was picking up a lot of the concepts very quickly. I was gaining confidence more rapidly than I had done in the past when I'd been learning something new. I also realized that all of my prior life experiences were actually helping me learn new ones. How cool was that? Although the coaching I had done at previous employers was different from this new kind of coaching, I could apply some of my earlier insights and experiences to the new approach. What's more, this new learning curve – and the feeling of confidence that went with it – was not restricted to my service offerings, it applied to other parts of my business as well.

I realized that setting up programs at my former employer was similar to setting up a business of my own. Many of the processes and tools were similar, less complex in my case, but similar. Talk about cutting down on the learning curve! And what a confidence boost! It turns out I was somewhat of a quasi-intrapreneur in my former role, and that was helping me out now as a quasi-entrepreneur.

I understand now what people mean when they suggest we try to gain as much exposure to as many things as we can, because those things (experiences) may well benefit us in the future. I understand what people mean when they suggest not feeling badly when we change paths on the career or business front. Those experiences are not wasted and will often come in handy in some other way in the future. I was experiencing that first-hand in both launching my business and in exploring and developing my capabilities in my service offerings. Cool! To that end, my new definition of change includes learning new things while leveraging the learnings of my past in order to learn and grow even faster. Wow! New experiences. Trying new things on for size. Bring it on!

April 2016. A Cocktail Party with No Booze. Are You Serious?

Mention the words "business development" and the word "cocktail" often comes up shortly thereafter. As my comfort level rose in meeting new people, I was also starting to feel more comfortable attending events where these new people tended to congregate, including cocktail parties. Although I was now feeling more comfortable at cocktail events, I still relied a little too much on some old friends of mine. Those old friends were the cocktails themselves, the ones of the alcoholic variety (a.k.a. my liquid courage). But this cocktail party was going to be my test. This was the first event I would attend since I had stopped drinking more than two drinks on any one occasion.

Well, not only did I enjoy the evening, I had so much fun connecting with people that I was the last to leave. I shut the place down. The hosts will probably order more San Pellegrino next time. Not only did I get to connect with a lot of former colleagues and meet new people, I actually remember what I said to them. I was actually present during our conversations. It turned out that learning new things about people and sharing ideas with them gave me as much of a buzz as booze had in the past. WOW, that was an unexpected and pleasant surprise!

June 2016. Storyteller Dave, Part 1. The Writer: My First Blog. Just Do It. Push the Button.

It was fast becoming time to write up or shut up. More like write something up or shut up (stop telling everyone that I was a writer, a storyteller). My Inner Critic kept reminding me that, although I prominently mentioned that writing was one of my service offerings, I had yet to write anything. While he was at it, my Inner Critic reminded me that I had tried writing articles and POVs (Points-of-View) in some of my former roles and I had not enjoyed the experience. None of my writing had ever even seen the light of day. They had ended up in the graveyard of my c: drive, in some unmarked folder. So, what was I thinking here? Coaching? Okay. Professional speaking? Maybe. Writing? Are you serious? What's with that? You can't write. At least nothing that anyone in their right mind would want to read. Besides, everyone is so busy these days. Do they even have time to read what you have to say?

Fortunately, my Inner Coach decided to weigh in and suggested I give it a try. "Just do it, Dave! Make the theory real." All right. Fair enough. So that's what I decided to do. For my first blog, I picked a topic that wasn't too radical. Searching for soulmates and dealing with clinical depression would have to wait. I decided on a safe path: I would write about dream jobs. I would come up with a "Top 5" list of the criteria for a dream job and post it on LinkedIn.

Things went well at first. I wrote it. I found a picture. I figured out, after some trial and error, how to post something on LinkedIn, and then I locked and loaded it all into the template. I was ready to push the "publish" button when my Inner Critic reappeared. "Don't do it, Dave.

Everyone on the planet will see it! This isn't your area of expertise! You haven't researched this enough, etc., etc., etc." Then my Inner Coach jumped in and told me to hit the button. "Don't listen to him, Dave. Hit the button! Hit the publish button!" They duked it out for quite a while until, finally, I just did it. I hit the publish button and posted my first blog. And guess what? I didn't die on the spot. I didn't get any nasty comments. No one challenged my ideas. Then again, how could they? They were my ideas. Did I get hundreds of likes and comments and clients from that post? No. But, boy, did it ever feel good! I enjoyed it so much that I could hardly wait to post my next blog.

For my second blog, I thought I would try to inspire others to make some changes to their habits in order to lead healthier lives, so I decided to write a blog on how my healthier approach to life had resulted in me losing 100 pounds of fat. Well, guess who showed up again? My Inner Critic. "Your blogs are way too long. No one will read them!" Hmmm. He might have a point there. I even Googled it, and he was right. My blogs were much longer than the average, but I was enjoying the writing and my approach, so I decided to continue with what I now refer to as my long-winded rants.

I could always summarize my blogs later and provide a link to the more detailed blog, but, for now, I was writing them for me. I would soon find out I was writing for some others who liked my style of sharing just about everything – and not holding much back, an approach that scared me a bit at first. I was sharing some pretty personal stuff. What would my family and friends and colleagues think? What would the world think? After all, once I posted the blogs, I was sharing them with the world. I hope you've been steering me in the right direction, Inner Coach.

I got some feedback on that front early on. I was driving my then 11-year-old son to camp one day, and I mentioned I had posted my blog on eating healthier the previous day. Without batting an eyelash, he asked if he could borrow my cell phone, looked it up and read it. "Not bad, Dad. I'll give you a nine out of ten. I'm deducting a point because you mentioned your son in the blog, but you didn't include my name." Not bad feedback on my second blog, if I do say so myself! And, for those of you who have not yet met my son, he has quite the memory and whenever I'm tempted to cheat on the nutrition front, he reminds me of that blog and suggests I might want to consider a healthier choice. He keeps me honest! Oh! And, by the way, his name is Shayne.

And, regarding the length of my blogs, here is some feedback from one of my first blog readers:

"Dave, very nice job on the 'Let's Talk' blog[28]. First, that is BY FAR the longest blog post I have ever read. But it is engaging and keeps you moving with an interesting short quip style. It is likely also the most honest and intimate blog I have ever read. Glad to see how much you are loving your new role/purpose in life..."

These were awesome words of encouragement! Take that, Inner Critic!

April 2017. Storyteller Dave, Part 2: The Motivational Speaker. Under the Glare of the Spotlights.

Okay, so it's been a year since I started blogging and my book is taking shape. It seemed like I was writing a book every time I corresponded with a client or contact. I enjoyed sharing and storytelling that much!

With the writing moving along nicely, it was now time to tackle professional speaking. That one was a little scarier. It's one thing to push a "publish" button, and quite another to get up in front of a live audience. How was I going to pull the trigger on that one?

Well, I got my chance. The local chapter of CAPS (Canadian Association of Professional Speakers) that I joined had sent out an email looking for eight volunteers to speak for seven minutes each at an upcoming event. The minute the newly-forged "Captain Courageous" read that email, he immediately hit the reply button and volunteered. He responded so quickly that neither his Inner Coach nor his Inner Critic could get a word in edgewise. I guess he was starting to get into the habit of taking on things that would have once been outside his comfort zone!

If you'd like to see how I did, take a peek in the motivational speaker section on my website[29]. Was I perfect? No. Did I bring the house down? No. Did I inspire anyone in the room to live a healthier lifestyle (the topic of my speech)? Who knows? That's their decision and not mine. I did my best. I put my best foot forward, despite not being able to see my audience because of the glare of the spotlights. Best of all, I just did it. I followed through with a commitment to myself. Captain Courageous just got up there and did it. It sure boosted my confidence!

SO, WHAT DID I LEARN?

How did I make change EASYer on myself ☺ (or not ☹)?

Self-confidence begets courage? Or, is it courage begets self-confidence? It's a chicken-or-egg kind of thing. I had been spending so much time out of my comfort zone trying new things during this period of self-transformation that I can't remember which came first, but I do know that one fed off the other.

And, here's another piece of the puzzle to ponder...My coach brought it up recently during a group discussion on ways of making things EASYer on myself in developing Self-Esteem. Self-esteem sounds pretty similar to self-confidence, so I was all ears. One way of doing it, apparently, is by following through on our commitments to ourselves. There's a lot of research to back up the importance of that one. Interesting concept. Following through on our commitments to ourselves. Hmmm.

Following through sounds a lot like perseverance, the way I was trying to find my mojo. It also blends in well with my "just do it", a.k.a. "just try it out", a.k.a. "just try it on for size" approach. After all, trying something in the first place takes a personal commitment. And a little courage, as well. Oh, no! Back to the chicken-and-egg thing! Oh, well. At least they're all related, so back to my original lesson learned: just give it a try! Take the plunge! That's where it all seems to start. But don't forget to keep at it. ☺

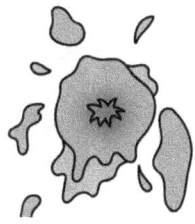

That was all about me. What about YOU?

What are you doing to make your journey of change EASYer on yourself? ☺ (or not ☹)?

Are you making commitments to yourself?

_____

_____

Are you following through on your commitments?

_____

_____

If the answer is "No," what's stopping you?

_____

_____

If the answer is, "Yes," are you doing it often enough?

_____

_____

Chapter 20: Having Fun along the Way!

Passion is energy. Feel the power that comes from focusing on what excites you.

Oprah Winfrey

This is a photo I took on my way to one of my hang-outs. One of my re-energizing hang-outs. The hang-out is a bench, in a park near my house. Fresh air, nice view, and a nice little walk to get there. Hard to beat! Although, it is a little cold in winter. ☺ Best of all, it's quite flexible. This re-energizing hang-out works just as well whether I'm honouring my need to re-energize by myself or with others. The bench holds up to three people comfortably. And there's plenty of standing room for others. How convenient is that?! I can re-energize alone or with others.

Winter, Spring and Summer of 2017. Connecting – Part 1: Sharing and Caring. Connecting with Others.

When it's time to identify ways in which I come up with my energy, it doesn't take me long, once I decide to put my mind to it. I can identify two key sources. One is spending quality time with myself; the other is spending quality time with others. I find that they are both very important. I have trouble having one without the other. And, I must admit, I have yet to find the sweet spot between the two, but I'm looking. Although I may never find the exact sweet spot, the level of self-awareness I'm gaining around what gives me my energy, and what takes it away, has been a real game-changer (life-changer). And, while I haven't yet found the ideal mix, I have found that, if I go too long without connecting with others, I start losing energy, and fast. To that end, even though these two parts are out of order chronologically, I've decided to tackle connecting with others first, in what I'm calling "Part 1" of this chapter and, then, I'll tackle connecting with myself in "Part 2." That is how important I now realize connecting with others is for me.

You'd think I'd have realized the power that social connectedness brought to energizing me when I went without it during my social isolationist days, but it's only recently that I've come to realize how powerful connecting with others can be. I see now that trying to tune everything and everyone else out during my clinical depression days was not a great approach when it came to figuring out how to energize myself. It was only later, when I was coming out of that funk, when I was starting to re-connect with people, that I realized how important the energy I received from connecting with others was to me.

And, by connecting with others, I mean, a lot of others. I was connecting with clients and potential clients; I was connecting with peers; I was connecting with my blog readers. I had so many connections I could only keep track of it all in a spreadsheet. I was sharing all kinds of material. I was sharing all kinds of ideas. And it seemed that the more I shared, the more people shared back with me. I was learning and growing just as much, if not more, than the people I was trying to help. Learning and growing (my Value #2 out of a possible 502) along with others. What an energizer!

I was amazed at how excited I was in the mornings. I would get out of bed and check the overnight messages from my LinkedIn and Facebook contacts. I was surprised at how energized I felt when I sent out some of my own. I was even squeezing in time to connect and share even more while on the bike at the gym. The more I shared with others, the more energized I felt. Leadership development. Share away! Improving communication. Share away! Increasing your level of energy. By all means, share away! Before I knew it, the shy, sales-averse Captain Comfort Zone was spending almost all of his time connecting with people and less and less time building the tools and processes needed to support his new business. Oops. It was time to refocus my energy. I needed to spend more time creating my tools, so I decided to go offline for a while and set them up. I would reconnect again later. That's just what I did. I went offline. And that's when I first started to notice it.

I noticed I was losing energy. Slowly at first but, then, I noticed I wasn't as excited to get up in the morning. What was going on? Well, what was going on was that I was realizing that I get a lot of my energy from sharing and connecting with others. Seems like I had over-vectored on the tool-building front. Oops! I might want to mix it up a bit more moving forward. Luckily for me, I was listening to my feelings and not tuning them out. I also knew myself a lot better. Sharing ideas was one of my Top Five Strengths. Learning by interacting with others is how I grow, also one of my top values. And here I was, cutting myself off from people. Yikes!

I know better now. I had tried isolating myself from others in the past and I sure didn't like the fit. Apparently, I'm not alone on the connection side of things. At my coaching school, we were taught nine guiding principles. Guess what came in at #4? "People grow from connection. Connecting is the wellspring of creativity. Collaboration is the conduit for enhancing people's strengths."[30] Wow! Growth! Creativity! Enhancing our strengths! Very cool! So, now, if you don't mind, I have some connecting to do.

Winter, Spring and Summer of 2015. Connecting – Part 2: My ME Time. Connecting with ME.

Somewhere along the path of my self-transformation from Captain Comfort Zone to Captain Courageous, I think that my passions got the better of me. All of a sudden, this person who was once a shy and quiet and more introverted guy had become what at first appeared to be a really extroverted guy. This was a huge personality change! It almost felt weird. My level of extroversion almost seemed more transformational to me than my recent 100-pound weight loss. That apparent personality change, more than anything else, really had me questioning whether I had become someone else through this mid-life self-transformation, or if I were reverting to who I had once been.

I remember taking a self-assessment on levels of introversion versus extroversion as part of a series of business development workshops I was facilitating around that time. When I asked the participants to separate into two groups based on their respective preferences, I joined the side with the more extroverted people. How weird was that? Then, something even weirder happened. One of the women in the more introverted group volunteered to share some information on what it was like to be more introverted. She was so passionate as she was sharing that information with us, that no one could get a word in edgewise. She was so excited and energized that she was almost standing on her chair. Her voice was loud and clear, and her passion was coming through in spades. What a difference passion can make in communicating with others, at least for a specific period of time. Either that or she had not answered the questions to the self-assessment correctly. Her passion just seemed to trump her introverted nature at that moment and things took off from there.

Hmmm. Maybe I wasn't as newly-extroverted as I thought? Maybe my new-found passion for what I was doing, and how I was going about doing it, was contributing to this new-found level of sharing my thoughts with others? It got me thinking. Was I as extroverted as I now thought I was? Is connecting with others really where I get most of my energy?

It was a very close friend who challenged me on that point as I was setting out as the newly-discovered Super-Extroverted Dave. She told me that she thought I wasn't as extroverted as I thought I was. Hmmm. Food for thought? It took me a while, and a lot of self-discovery, and a lot of trying things out but, now, I believe she was right. I believe that a lot of my increased level of extroversion was brought about by a huge increase in my level of passion at certain times.

I had become so passionate about what I was doing and sharing that my introverted self just seemed to fade away. The more I connected and shared, the more the momentum and passion and desire to share would become. But then something else happened. More of a feeling than an event. I felt as if I had hit a wall. My energy and my desire to connect with others would just seem to go away. That was usually on Friday night or Saturday morning. At first, I wasn't sure what was happening, but I soon figured it out. I needed some quiet time with my close family members and, also, with just little old me. I had come to realize that, not only did I want some time alone to recharge, I needed it.

Good thing I didn't throw out my movies because, apparently, I still might have some use for them, just not as many, and not as often. Oh! And the time I was able to spend just connecting with myself when I was alone? Well, what can I say? It turned out to be a huge energizer. Not to mention an important time for self-reflection. Connecting with myself and connecting with others, Part 1 and Part 2. You can't have one without the other. At least, I can't.

SO, WHAT DID I LEARN?

How did I make change EASYer on myself ☺ (or not ☹)?

So, now that I have realized that I require a balance between connecting with others and connecting with myself, have I found that sweet spot? Not yet. Will I ever find it? I doubt it, but I'm not going to stress about it. At least now, with my new-found level of self-awareness around where I get my energy, I have a better sense of when my energy is starting to wane and when it's time to switch gears as to what I'm doing and who I'm doing it with. Sharing and caring with others and sharing and caring with myself, either way, I can get energized and have FUN while doing it! I don't how I can make it any EASYer on myself than that. ☺

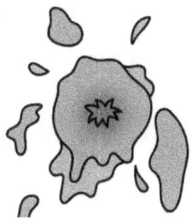

That was all about me. What about YOU?

What are you doing to make your journey of change EASYer on yourself? ☺ (or not ☹)?

What gives you energy?

_____

_____

And, what takes it away?

_____

_____

Have you experimented with your energy sources and drainers in order to find your balance?

_____

_____

What would be possible in your life if you had more energy?

_____

_____

Chapter 21: Finding My Heart and My Soul

Do the right thing and your heart sings.
Unknown

Whoville! Talk about an appropriate place to find one's WHO! It's the reason I have a picture of Whoville on the cover of my "WHO are YOU" workbook. In this case, Whoville was also an appropriate place to find my heart. I found out, through my new-found level of self-awareness, that the Grinch wasn't the only dude who had a heart that was three sizes too small. ☹

March 2014. Communications 101. It Takes Two to Tango.

It was during one of our earlier sessions together that my relationship counselor, an accredited psychologist and marriage counselor, shared with me what has become one of my favorite analogies, "Communication is to a relationship what water is to a plant." Apparently, it applies to all kinds and types of relationships; communication between romantic couples and non-romantic ones, communication between parents and children, communication between employers and employees, and so on. Communicating sounds like the polar opposite of what I was doing during my time spent isolating myself during my career rut and, truth be told, my long-held tendency not to share my thoughts, concerns and frustrations with others. For some reason, I thought that keeping my concerns and frustrations to myself was the logical thing to do. I figured that, if I kept things to myself, I could avoid conflict and/or hurting someone's feelings. By keeping things to myself, maybe (I was hoping) the issues would go away or become less sensitive or less annoying over time. Kind of like the radiation levels in plutonium diminishing over time and, in the case of radiation, it takes millennia.

I realize now that rarely happened on the relationship side of things. At least not for me. When I failed to communicate, things did not right themselves over time. Things did not go away. Things just got worse. And by failing to communicate, I include both failing to communicate with others and with myself. I am aware of my communication shortcomings now and my intention is to work on them, and that's what I have been doing, especially my listening skills. And, given my new-found belief in awareness being nine-tenths of the battle, I believe that my future on the communication front is looking pretty rosy.

Speaking of awareness, it dawned on me recently that improving my communications skills is only half the battle. Apparently, communication is a two-way street. I can work on my communication skills all I want but, if the person I am trying to communicate with is not willing or able to do so as well, it will all be for naught. Have you ever tried having a conversation with a chair? Or with a rock? Or with me, in my nasty days?

One of my new favorite sayings is that "it takes two to tango." If you don't believe me, try communicating with someone who doesn't communicate with you in return. See how long you can keep that up and let me know how it goes. Picture this! Picture a really well-meaning, caring and loving gardener watering a plant every day. The only problem is that the gardener does not get water in return. After a while, the gardener, just like a plant with no water, will start to get very thirsty and will eventually just shrivel up. Shriveling up is not much fun. It can be quite painful. Take it from me. I've been there. So, time to take some tango lessons. Like all lessons, it boils down to practice, practice, practice. And focus, focus, focus. When my son tries to tell me something, I've found that the effectiveness of the communication is much higher when I look at him while he's talking. Drying the dishes can wait. And I'm going to be more selective in choosing my tango partners. My preference and focus will be on ones who are also open to continuing to improve their dancing (communication) skills as well.

March 2016: Emotions 101. Failing My EQ Test. Yes, Martians Have Emotions, Too.

Emotional Intelligence. I don't remember when I first came across the concept but, when I did, I decided that the best way to dive in and explore it was, you guessed it, another self-assessment. I came across one in the book *Emotional Intelligence 2.0*[31] by Travis Bradberry and Jean Graves. One of the reviews on the cover touts it as "the world's most popular emotional intelligence test." And, besides, it also included an endorsement from the Dalai Lama on the cover. How could I go wrong?

So, I took the self-assessment and, when I got my score back, I quickly realized that something was wrong. I wasn't sure what, but my score was terrible. My overall emotional intelligence score (my EQ test score) was 55, which was described in the book as "a concern that I must address." And I had shortcomings and "concerns" on both emotional intelligence dimensions: being self-aware of my own emotions (EQ Dimension 1) and being aware of the emotions of others (EQ Dimension 2). Another double whammy. Okay, what to do? Hmmm.

Luckily for me, the *Emotional Intelligence 2.0* book came with a cheat sheet that included what were referred to as "the five core emotions": Happy, Sad, Angry, Afraid, and Ashamed.[32] I was almost being encouraged to cheat by being given the cheat sheet, and so I did. I photocopied the cheat sheet and carried it around with me. Here was this 50-year old Martian wandering around with his "emotions" cheat sheet that he would pull out and refer to whenever he encountered an emotional reaction from himself or someone else. Before I knew it, I started to get a better handle on how I was feeling. The cheat sheet helped, and so did some of the exercises in the emotional intelligence book. But, what really helped the most was summoning the courage to share and discuss my emotions with others. Yes, Captain Courageous had shown up in the latter part of those days and, unlike Captain Comfort Zone, he was not afraid to initiate a conversation on emotions. It was more difficult to share them with guys than gals at first (must be a Martian thing) but soon he (me) became quite inclusive in engaging with people. Engaging with others and engaging with himself.

If I was feeling down, instead of ignoring how I was feeling, I would pull out my cheat sheet. First, I tried to identify how I was feeling; then I tried to figure out what was making me feel that way. Once I had a better sense of what was causing my emotional reaction, I was in a better position to do something about it, which sometimes included just letting it pass while at other times it meant exploring it further. And by trying to figure my emotions out, I soon discovered I had more success by using my heart than by using my head. I had spent enough time in my head in the past. It was time to let my heart do some of the connecting. The heart is a muscle and, like all muscles, if you don't use it, it shrinks and atrophies. Kind of like what happened to the Grinch in the book and movie, *How the Grinch Stole Christmas*. In my case, it felt like someone had stolen my heart. Not only was it several sizes too small, it seemed to have gone AWOL. I was like the Tin Man in *The Wizard of Oz*. I had no heart. What had the Wizard done with it, I wondered? It was time to start using it again. After all, that's where we feel things, in the heart, and not in the head.

I continue to make progress on the emotional intelligence front. And, while my score continues to improve, I remind myself that there are still things I should work on. So, work on them I do, by practising them. This time, though, I practise with others. After all, it takes two to tango. This time, I will lead with my heart and not my head. These days, every now and then, instead of asking people "How are you today?" I ask, "How are you feeling today?" And that includes me. Yes, asking myself, "Dave, how are you feeling today?" Wow! Feeling my feelings. That was a new idea!

June 2016: Relationships 101.

The area of relationships is another area where the tango analogy seems to apply. Unfortunately for me, "relationship management" was the category of the "emotional intelligence" self-assessment in which I scored the lowest. Yikes! You'd think that someone who had been the program director for a relationship development program in a previous role would have a better grasp of relationships than that. Sounds like someone needs to take some tango lessons.

Speaking of relationship development programs, when I think back to that program, one word often comes to mind. That word is "Trust." Hmmm. Interesting. I can't help but think that, if you trust someone, it will make things a lot EASYer when communicating with them. When I think of sharing emotions with someone, really opening up the kimono and sharing one's true feelings, I can't help but think that trust is a huge enabler on that front as well. To that end, one could surmise that trust is an important aspect of developing and maintaining relationships. And you know what they say about trust, "it is hard to gain, but easy to lose."

When it comes to developing trusted relationships, there are two other words that come to mind. It was time to revisit my list of values to see if Honesty were on there somewhere. And while I am at it, I'll take a look to see where Authenticity is located. Trying to be someone you're not. Trying to come across as someone you're not. That was a show-stopper on the relationship front. Good thing I've decided to find myself. Truly find myself. Find Dave. It might have taken me a while but, you know what they say, "It's never too late to learn a new dance step." In my case, the tango, the relationship tango.

July 2016: Spirituality 101 and the Top 12 List of Indicators of Spiritual Awakening

Spirituality. That was a biggy! I had recently connected on many fronts, including my heart. Was I now ready to connect with my soul? My spiritual self? Spirituality, I could barely spell the word in those days, let alone understand what it meant. And part of that ignorance was a lack of desire to understand it. I had better things to do than yoga, meditation and visiting the Dalai Lama on some secluded mountain in Tibet. I did eventually give yoga a try. I was introduced to it by some close friends. I still enjoy a session on occasion, but I haven't found it to be the life-changing practice that others claim it is for them. Not yet. Meditation? I tried it but, once again, not for me, at least not for now. On the visiting Tibet front? That one has yet to hit my bucket list. Despite not connecting on all of those supposed "spiritual" fronts, I have finally decided to start exploring my spiritual side. Once again, I owe my spiritual awakening or, at least my current understanding of it, to a list. In this case, the list was a Top 12 List, appropriately named *The 12 Symptoms of Spiritual Awakening*[33]. I started to read them and guess what I realized? Apparently, as part of my journey of self-discovery and self-transformation, I had awoken on the spiritual side of things and not even realized it.

I was starting to do the things on the list! Not just a few of them, but most of them! And it felt good. How could it not? I was replacing a lot of my bad habits with good habits. I was worrying less, judging myself and others less, enjoying moments more, feeling more connected to others and nature. Not to mention one of my favourites – frequent attacks of smiling. What can I say, the accountant in me wanted to get more ROI (Return on Investment) from finally having taken care of my teeth and getting back that "Colgate smile." At the same time, I was replacing habits that had once drained me of energy with ones that provided energy. I was replacing habits that disconnected me from others with habits that connected me to others. I was appreciating things more. I was enjoying the moment more and worrying less and less about the past. I was starting to worry less about the future, as well.

Wow! If this is what it feels like to connect with my soul and with other souls, I could get used to it. And, I much prefer the focus on the positive rather than the negative. It's a lot more energizing! So, here's a thumbs-up for spirituality and connecting with one's soul. And, speaking of souls, maybe I'm ready to connect with my soulmate? After all these tango lessons, I think I'm ready for a tango. A tango with my soulmate.

SO, WHAT DID I LEARN?

How did I make change EASYer on myself ☺ (or not ☹)?

Connecting with others and myself, and not just via the head, meant bringing a whole arsenal to the task: both my heart (one that had recently grown at least three times its size ☺), and my soul. Turns out that my emotions and my emotional intelligence are in my heart and in my soul, and not in my head. Ooops! It took me a while to figure that one out, but better late than never.

And, the Grinch and I are not the only dudes who've been missing out on the magic of these areas. ☹ From one Martian to my fellow Martians, if you're looking for ways for making and maintaining change EASYer on yourselves, the Grinch and I highly recommend taking a peek at your hearts and your souls. Oh! And don't forget, explore your emotions. Take it from another dude, in this case Mr. Spock from the TV show *Star Trek*: given the link between understanding and playing to our emotions, and the resulting level of our emotional intelligence, it would seem to be the logical thing to do. ☺

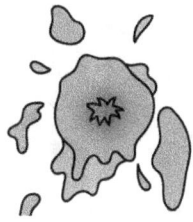

That was all about me. What about YOU?
What are you doing to make your journey of change EASYer on yourself? ☺ (or not ☹)?

Is your EQ where you want it to be?

_____

What about the health of your current relationships? The ones that really matter.

_____

What's one thing you can do today to get a better grip on your EQ?

_____

_____

What's one thing you can do to reconnect with someone important on the relationship front?

_____

_____

Oh! And how are you at doing the tango?

_____

200 MONDAYS *don't have to* **SUCK!**

Chapter 22: Finding My Soulmate

*I love it, Dave! Captain Courageous is cute. ☺
There's something amazing about people who
are not afraid to just be themselves.*

A very beautiful woman in my life

Soulmate. Noun. A person ideally suited to another as a close friend or romantic partner.

It took me a while to come up with the final naming convention for my fourth Life Quadrant. It also took time to start spending time in it; quality time, that is. One of my "Top 3" newly discovered love languages.

January 2015 to January 2018. Defining My Soulmate Quadrant. From Theory to Reality.

If I had five cents for every time someone told me that soulmates don't exist, I would be a very wealthy Martian by now. "Dave, get with it. Soulmates are like leprechauns, they don't exist. You're going to have to settle for less!" Oops, I thought to myself, I had better rename my soulmate quadrant then. Maybe Life Partner? Or Better Half? Or Spouse? Or Settling for Less? Well, I did rename it. And rename it again. Back and forth, between "soulmate" and one of the "other" names, often based on a recent conversation with someone, or after reading an article on the subject. How many times did it change? I don't remember, but it a was a lot. I now realize it was hard to stick up for something – i.e. the concept of the soulmate – that, at the time, was more theory than reality to me. Because I was planning to devote a whole one of my Life Quadrants to it, I felt it might be worth exploring. I had spent enough time exploring this topic through the lenses of other people, it was time to explore it through mine.

Life Quadrand #4: My SOULMATE
NOW OPEN FOR BUSINESS!

SOULMATE

Date nights	Chemistry	Love languages
Fun	Quality 1-on-1 time	Cooking together
Words of affirmation	Romantic weekends	"In the flow!"
Communication	All the other non-romantic things that we do together	Going for walks
Trust		Filling each other's buckets
Physical touch		

To make a really long story a bit shorter, I did some exploring. I also decided to name this Life Quadrant my Soulmate Quadrant and, this time around, I was determined to stick to my guns and my naming convention. These are the stories of how I took my fourth Life Quadrant from theory to reality and, at the same time, allowed me to meet a lot of very beautiful and caring women, including the one who is currently exploring that quadrant with me. I must say, I'm enjoying her company. A lot! But I'm getting ahead of myself.

January 2015. Happy big 5-0! Ready to Start Dating again.

Start dating again? I had barely dated before. Before getting married, my longest relationship with a woman had lasted two months. That had happened twice. Before that, the record had been two weeks. I had had many shorter relationships as well. Lots. The minute that things turned south, I was out. John Gray, the author of *Men are from Mars, Women are from Venus* refers to this as the "rubber band effect".[34] When I started to get close to a woman, my rubber band would pull me back. In fact, it would pull me so far back that I would back right out of the relationship and, on more than one occasion, regret having done so.

Now, here I was, ready to hit the dating scene again. This was after my self-imposed, two-year hiatus on dating, during which I took care of a few things in my other Life Quadrants, the ones labelled "Me," "My Kids" and "My Career." I was still working on my transition in role at my former employer, so dating and meeting women had had to take a back seat until I had a better handle on that one. Well, the wait was finally over, as I told my best friend over beer celebrating my big 5-0 and the recent big drop in my weight. I was primed and ready to go. "Hmmm," my friend said, "I might have someone in mind. I'll put her in contact with you. If she's interested, the two of you can take it from there."

Boy, was she in for a treat. Little did she realize she was about to be introduced to someone I now refer to as Super Dave. He was, shall we say, a legend in his own mind. Things were going well for Super Dave in those days. Things were finally going well for him at work, he was coming to grips with the demands of single parenthood, and he was even looking good in his new wardrobe. But, there were a couple of other areas that Super Dave had not yet mastered. So, unless possessing the listening skills of a chair and the emotional intelligence of a rock were super powers, Dave had some more work to do on himself. Was he aware of that at the time? Not! He was so excited about his new look on the outside that he had forgotten about all the stuff that he had to look after on the inside. And he was about to find out that his journey of self-discovery and self-transformation still had a way to go, and he had a lot of work to do. But, luckily for him, he was going to have the opportunity to do some of that work with a very beautiful and very special person.

When it comes to being set up, it turned out my best friend had chosen well. Best friends tend to do that. It might have something to do with how well they know your values and the type of person you are. The lady he had selected and I were duly introduced. At the time, I thought that my life transition was pretty much done. Health and wellness-wise, maybe it was, but on the relationship front, especially relationships with women, I was not even close to being through the tunnel. And, I was all set to crash and burn. So much for my super powers. Welcome to the dating zone. Oh, oh! I feel that elastic band starting to stretch. Time to bolt.

But then, something strange happened. I didn't bolt. I stayed in the relationship. Even when things got a little rocky, I stayed. I stayed, and I learned. I stayed, and I grew. I grew as a person, and I grew as a Martian. I learned about relationships, and I learned about myself. This lovely lady even taught me how a Martian can listen to someone from Venus. It was when we were walking in the park together one night, that she taught me the concept of listening. Quite the feat. In those days, my nickname was "David Walker Talker" and not "David Walker Listener." She had the coolest way of conveying that message to me. I would love to share the approach with you but, as Tom Hanks mentions in *Saving Private Ryan*, "I think that I will keep that one to myself."

I had no idea that we (men) were supposed to just listen at times, and not try to fix things. Interesting! You hear that, Super Dave? Not everyone is interested in hearing about how you fixed yourself, and how others should emulate you. We are pleased to hear that your approach worked for you, but that is you. That doesn't mean that it will, or should, work for everybody else. Okay, thanks for the feedback. Noted for future reference.

In the end, it turned out that our timing wasn't right. At least not right in my finding-my-soulmate department, and not right in her finding-her-soulmate department. But, the timing was perfect for meeting someone who had the patience to help me take on another transition. In this case, a transition from rubber-band man to someone who really appreciates the company of a beautiful, loving and caring woman. For that, she will always have a special place in my heart.

November 2015. Taking a First Pass at My Online Dating Profile. Un-Authentic Me.

It took me a few hours, but I had done it. After procrastinating for I don't know how long, I had put together the first draft of my online dating profile and it was not that bad, if I do say so myself. But, I figured that I might want to get a second opinion and, who better than my relationship counselor. Oh! Did I forget to mention to you that this is how single people meet other single people these days? Online? Hence, my online profile. Well, I shared it with her and she was not impressed, not at all. "Dave, this isn't you! What about your kids? There's no mention of your kids. You love your kids. They are such a big part of your life, yet you don't even mention them." To which I replied, "I only have them one week out of two, if a woman doesn't like kids, she can still be with me part-time." What kind of soulmate is a part-time soulmate? Then she challenged me again, "Dave, what are all these activities you list as things that you like to do? Have you even tried any of them?" Yikes! Okay, sounds like it's time to head back to the drawing board, or, in this case, version 2.0 of my dating profile. Got it. Any other advice? "Yes. Just be you, Dave. Be the authentic you."

November 2016. Exploring the Top Traits of My Soulmate. In Theory, at Least. As a Start.

A year had passed since I had posted my first profile on a couple of dating sites but, let's just say I was struggling a bit to make the time (and find the courage) to reach out to prospective soulmates. For some reason, Captain Courageous had not yet shown up in this, his fourth Life Quadrant. There wasn't much action, or progress, in making the theory real. So, I came up with an interim approach. I would explore the topic through one of my blogs. I am giving myself full credit for tackling this topic as my fifth blog, "Dave's Top 5 List: Top 5 10 Traits of MY Soulmate."[35] I even elicited the help of several denizens of the planet Venus. I see now that connecting with a couple of Martians might have been insightful, too, but it might also have proven more difficult, since the topic is not something we Martians like to chat about openly. Ironically, this blog turned out to be the only one of my "Top 5 list blogs" that turned into a Top 10 List. This was a sure sign that I was having trouble identifying the top traits. I won't repeat the whole blog here. Feel free to read it at your leisure on my website, but guess which trait came in at #1? I'll give you a hint. It starts with "C."

If you guessed Communication, you're right. Oh, and our good friend, Trust? Right up there as well. And being Authentic? That one came across loud and clear from all of my female collaborators. Supposedly, if I portray myself as someone I'm not, I'll attract women looking for someone else. They're not going to stay very long with me nor, supposedly, will I want them to.

Oh, and one more concept to share from one of my collaborators. "Things will just flow," she told me. Interesting. "And how will I know when that happens?" I asked. Her reply was, "You'll just know." Okay. Well, I hadn't felt that one before, but it sounded kind of interesting, so I was looking forward to it. But first, there was one small detail to work out, and that was actually reaching out to women in the first place. There couldn't be a whole lot of "flowing" until I started connecting. Captain Courageous, where are you?

Winter and Spring of 2017. Making the Theory Real. Hitting the Dating Sites. From Fear to Fun.

Spring was in the air. Love was in the air. But, for some reason, I didn't have a lot of messages in my dating site inbox. This was not too surprising, given that I hadn't sent out many messages, or any message, for that matter. Funny, I'd recently developed the courage to reach out to just about anyone to see how I could help them as a coach and storyteller and I was actually enjoying it very much. So, what was stopping me from doing the same and feeling the same when reaching out in my quest for my potential soulmate?

I had tried everything to make it EASYer on myself. Scheduling time in the morning when I was most energized. Scheduling time on the weekends when I didn't have the kids, etc., but to no avail. Then, one day, it just seemed to click. I think it was the day a whole bunch of things just clicked. Although I wasn't doing a lot of reaching out, I was doing some and, so far, the results were way more positive than negative, which I found encouraging. More evidence, as I call it, that action results in good things happening – when I persisted. Some women were even courageous enough to reach out to me. And guess what? We seemed to share similar values. Hmmm. I guess my authentic dating profile was a good idea after all. Thanks, relationship counselor! Before I knew it, I was experiencing even more positive consequences from my actions. Before I knew it, I was experiencing the "M" word – Momentum. I was starting to have fun. I was no longer dreading the thought of going on the dating site. It no longer felt like a chore. I was actually checking my messages at the end of the day when I had the least amount of energy, and it gave me energy!

To top it all off, one of my Venusian friends let me in on a little secret: women like men who write. I realize she might have been sharing that thought through her own lens, but who cares? I was now into writing, so I was going to write. Suddenly I was no longer staring at profiles online and struggling to come up with a way to connect with them. I was now composing stories to share. Just like my blogs, it was up to the reader to choose to read it, or not. I felt good, often great, just sharing. And, just like my blogs, where I was excited to hit the "publish" button when I was ready to share, I was hitting the "send" button in my online dating application.

Just as I hypothesized in my blog, women who shared my values and appreciated my honesty and authenticity were the ones who reached out. The others did not. I even met a few women who, although we didn't become soulmates, later became friends. It sure beat the hell out of watching movies all by myself in my basement on weekends!

May 2017. It Takes Two to Tango. It also Takes Time to Tango. Quality Time.

Despite my new-found comfort in reaching out to women, there was one in particular who had my undivided attention. She had contacted me in the fall; my profile – my authentic one – resonated with her. Her name is Qita. We decided to meet, as friends at first, and share our respective stories and journeys and – wait for it – our values. It turned out that my values GPS was coming in handy after all. We had a lot of values in common, including learning and growth and a love of children (yes, the same children I did not include in my previous profile). Can you say "growth mindset"? She could.

We eventually decided to take our relationship to the next level. And it has been flowing ever since. And, by flowing, I mean across the board, especially on the communication front. I am now sharing my thoughts and feelings. All of them. Nothing is taboo and, so far, nothing nasty has happened. Just the opposite – a real trust has developed between the two of us.

Communication and trust. It seems like the advice in the blog was right. And best of all, as that Venusian contributor mentioned in the blog, it will "just feel right." So far, it does. Although we're still in the early days of this relationship, and time will ultimately determine if this is my soulmate or not, things are flowing. It feels right this time around, but there's just one little issue, more like a challenge. And that challenge is, wait for it, TIME. I've been juggling three Life Quadrants for the better part of three years now, and I'm an accountant, not a juggler. All of a sudden, the theory has become very real and I not only need to, but want to, make time in my life for someone else. What a reality check! Ready or not, the fourth Life Quadrant is now up and running. No more theory, Davey boy, it's real now. Date nights. Vacation time together. Just plain talking and spending time together. They all take time and I have a business to run, and so does she. I have kids to take care of, and so does she. I have family and friends to connect with, and so does she. Four quadrants! Quality time in four quadrants! Can you say balance? Forget saying it, can you live it? Live it, day in and day out?

If we can put people on the moon, I'm confident we'll figure out a way to make this work. Notice I said WE, and not ME. Remember, it takes two to tango. It sounds like a little re-prioritization is in order. It sounds like it's time to change a few old routines and, maybe, start a few new ones. Where there's a will, there's a way. In this case, our will is our desire to spend time together, quality time. And guess what? We had both completed the "love languages" self-assessment a little while previously and, as it turns out, we both have one of the same primary love languages in common: "quality time." How cool is that?

SO, WHAT DID I LEARN?

How did I make change EASYer on myself ☺ (or not ☹)?

"Communication to a relationship is like water to a plant." I'm not sure who came up with that saying but I love it. And by communication, my hypothesis is that they meant open and honest communication. And that takes work, a lot of work, and a lot of courage, and a lot of trust. EASYer said than done when the initial stage of the relationship, the honeymoon phase or "Romantic Obsession" as Gary Chapman refers to it in *The 5 Love Languages*[36], is over. Whether at the end of that so-called honeymoon phase or a bit later on, a lot of people just seem to stop working on the communication front. And the results are not pretty.

According to an article by the American Psychological Association, "about 40 to 50 percent of married couples in the United States divorce. The divorce rate for subsequent marriages is even higher."[37] As I previously mentioned, if those statistics are not discouraging enough, just think of the relationships and marriages where people are still together but have really grown apart. They are physically together but not emotionally. Not a pretty picture ☹. It doesn't sound like a lot of work is happening on the communication front these days, at least not among a lot of couples. Maybe it's just me who feels this way, but it's funny how we hear lots of advice to take care of ourselves and take care of our kids and other family members but, there doesn't seem to be as strong a message to take care of our life partner and our relationship with our life partner. They often end up last. We will likely spend the most time with our partners relationship-wise over the course of our lives, yet they are often last on the relationship-maintenance front.

Well, here's to communication and communicating with our soulmate. You hear that, Qita?! I am committing to keeping the communication going post-honeymoon phase. I can't think of an EASYer way to maintain our relationship and also take it to the next level than to keep up the communication (watering our plant). ☺ But, remember, it takes two to tango. So, keep me honest. I promise to do the same with you. To do the same with you because I love you!

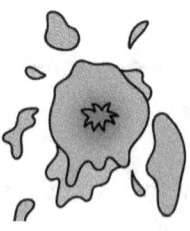

That was all about me. What about YOU?

What are you doing to make your journey of change EASYer on yourself? ☺ (or not ☹)?

How are things flowing in your Soulmate Quadrant?

_____

_____

Can you imagine how much richer life would be if you and your partner were maximizing your Soulmate Quadrant(s)?

_____

_____

Is it time for a little more quality time? Or more time for whatever your respective love languages are?

_____

_____

Can you book that in right now? Use a little imagination or use a lot!

_____

_____

Chapter 23:
Trying Really Hard to Maintain My Balance

Life is like riding a bicycle. To keep your balance, you must keep moving.

Albert Einstein

When I think of work-life balance, I picture a chair. In my case, because I have four Life Quadrants, I picture a four-legged chair. If one or more legs (quadrants) is broken or in need of repair, it's pretty tough to maintain my balance when sitting on that chair. When all four are synchronized and working well, it makes the balancing act a whole lot EASYer. But, that is often EASYer said than done.

Summer 2017. Finding My Discipline. Adding another Balancing Act to the Mix.

IDEATION. "People who are especially talented in the ideation theme are fascinated by ideas. They are able to find connections between seemingly disparate phenomena."[38] Coming up with ideas is one of my Top Five Strengthsfinder 2.0 strengths. Turns out, it is also a big part of my communication style. My communication style, according to the PCSI communication style framework, is that of a "Presenter"[39]." One of the strengths associated with the "Presenter" communication style is that this individual is "an idea factory." Another strength is that they know how to have fun. FUN![40] Wow! My new-found communication style! It was wonderful!

Are there any blind spot(s) associated with that communication style? Naturally! One of them is "poor operational follow-through."[41] Say what? You mean all of my ideas actually require follow-through? There are way too many of them! Even too many for my "strengthsfinder" Activator strength ("People who are especially talented in the activator strength can make things happen by turning thoughts into action"[42]) to balance things out. Yikes! I'm starting to realize why I often feel like I'm all over the place. All over the place, and all over my four Life Quadrants and, often, all over them all at the same time. Ever hear of the saying "trying to do too much in too little time?" Ever hear of "biting off more than you can chew?" Talk about a lack of presence! And, remember, there are only 168 hours in a week. Subtract 56 hours for sleep and there's not a lot of time left to squeeze in everything else I want to do. 168 hours in a week is not enough to pack in everything I want (and sometimes try) to do in a week. No wonder I was feeling a bit scattered, not to mention quite stressed on occasion. And the 168 hours is just for the fun stuff!

The un-fun stuff isn't included in the 168 hours. I was avoiding the un-fun stuff and letting it slide until it came back to haunt me – usually when I was in one of my other Life Quadrants. It was hard enough being present at any one time in this day and age of constant bombardment from texts and emails and other distractions. Having stuff from one Life Quadrant distract me while I was in another Life Quadrant wasn't doing much for my attempts to "be in the moment" either. What to do? In this case, I decided that finding balance among my Four Life Quadrants would require a little more balance in how I was managing them. And that balance came from embracing a bit more discipline. Fun was still going to dominate my thoughts and my dreams and my actions, but I was going to balance my actions with more discipline. And how exactly was I going to do that?

First, I would draw upon one of my other Top Five strengths, and that was Responsibility. People who possess this strength "take psychological ownership of what they say they will do."[43] Next, I would draw upon the functionality of my electronic calendar in order to start setting time aside to actually start doing both the things I wanted to do and the things I needed to do. I would use a colour-coding scheme to track them. I decided to use the colour red (the colour of my heart) for time with my sweetheart and yellow (the colour of the sun) for time with my family. My time at the office also had a colour. Remember, I was trying to limit myself to an average of 40 hours a week in my business quadrant, so what better way to keep myself honest than by tracking it? Sound a little anal as an approach? Maybe. But, hey, if it works, go with it!

Once my calendar was colour-coded, it was up to me to execute. I remember clearly one Monday in the summer of 2017. I was in a quaint little coffee shop in the country typing away on one of my blogs and drinking tea while listening to music with my earphones. I was focused. I was in the zone. I was in my business quadrant, in this case. Ideas were flowing. Words were flowing. My fingers were flying across the keys. And then it happened. A 15-minute calendar reminder popped up for 5:00 p.m. and the appointment was at another location. I had a date with my sweetheart – dinner, followed by a walk in the country. I quickly wrapped up what I was doing, packed my portable office into my carry-all and off I went to spend time in the next Life Quadrant. As it turned out, walking and talking were all that I did that evening. I did not think of business or the kids or the endless to-do's that had to get done. I was spending time with my sweetheart, quality time, one of our top love languages. She had shown up for our date, both physically and mentally, so it only seemed fair that I do likewise. Would I be as committed if the activities were less fun? That's where discipline comes in. Either I figure out a way to make activities fun, or I outsource them, or I just do them and get them out of the way. If they need to get done, I want them done. That way, when the next calendar invite pops up, I'll be ready to spend quality time on the activity; ready to spend quality time, whether it's just me enjoying some down time, or spending time with my children, or meeting with a client or potential client. I will be there. I will be present. Maybe not all the time but, with a little more discipline, most of the time.

January 19, 2018 until the Day I Die (Date TBD). Managing My Portfolio. My Balanced Portfolio.

If balance is all about continuing to move forward (and who am I to argue with Albert Einstein on that point), then the question I ask myself is "How do I continue to move forward while making things EASYer on myself?" In today's crazy, go-go culture, finding the balance between work, rest and play sounds about as easy as finding the Holy Grail. And finding the Holy Grail doesn't sound all that easy.

When I think of my desire to live a balanced lifestyle, I picture a guy standing on a chair, juggling. In this case, the juggler on that chair looks a lot like me. Not only can I picture him, I can picture him at various times during my recent life journey.

When I look back on my nasty period, there isn't a whole lot of juggling going on. The juggler is lying down, letting life pass him by. I don't see much of a chair supporting him, either. The legs of the chair are broken and in need of repair. A few years later, the chair has three legs and appears more stable. The juggler seems to enjoy tossing three balls in the air. He seems to be pretty good at it, too. He's also enjoying interactions with other jugglers along the way. Sometimes they even throw their balls back and forth to each other. A ball is dropped from time to time, but it's not bad. He's becoming a much better juggler.

Just recently, I took another look. The juggler is enjoying himself even more. And, even though the number of balls has increased to four, his juggling is improving. He looks even more stable on that chair, despite the extra ball. Maybe it's because his chair now has four legs, not three. Maybe it's because the chair is sturdy. Maybe that's because, not only has the juggler made repairs to the chair, he's been practising regularly; practising by himself and practising with the other people who are there to help the juggler pick up a ball when one hits the ground every now and then. Okay, maybe more than one gets dropped, and maybe that happens more than every once in a while. But, hey, have you ever tried to juggle? Have you ever tried to juggle four balls on a chair that was missing a leg or two? Or missing legs altogether? I have. I tried it during my nasty period and I didn't enjoy the experience. Moving forward into my second half of life, I've decided on a different approach.

For those of you who are already tiring of my overuse of analogies for leading a balanced lifestyle (e.g. juggling and chairs and riding bicycles), I have one more. I have called on "Dave the Accountant" a few times in the book to this point, but now I'm going to call on "Dave the Investment Portfolio Manager." I'm going to ask him to share his approach to managing a balanced portfolio (a.k.a. balanced life style).

Do you hear that, Portfolio Manager Dave? You might have screwed up the portfolio for your investment club in the past by putting all of your eggs in one basket, but here's your chance to improve. For the sake of us non-financial gurus, would you please share your approach?

Sure thing, Dave. Glad to help! Here's my three-step approach to maintaining (or at least trying to maintain) a balanced portfolio:

STEP 1: Choose the number and type of asset classes (or in this case, Life Quadrants) you would like to have in your portfolio. In your case, it sounds like, after having tried three quadrants for a while, you have settled on four.

STEP 2: Decide what you would like to put in each quadrant (in your case, what activities you would like to include in each). You'll be monitoring and changing them constantly so try not to choose too many. Some will go as planned and others will not. You'll want to adjust the mix accordingly. And remember to keep an eye on the objectives of your balanced portfolio (your values) when selecting what you do and, most importantly, who you do it with.

STEP 3: Monitor your progress. As long as your portfolio is active, you'll want to check up on it once in a while, to see if it's still balanced. If, for some reason, it's become unbalanced, you'll have to make some changes to WHAT you're doing, or HOW you're doing it or, most importantly, WHO you're doing it with.

There you go, Dave! How did you like my "Balancing Your Life Portfolio 101" course? Now, if you don't mind, I have some emails I need to get out by 3:55 p.m. Then I'm heading out to pick up the kids. We're going skating tonight. Finishing up the first draft of my book will have to wait until tomorrow. Two days and four chapters to go to finish in time for my fifty-third birthday. I'm celebrating it with the beautiful woman in my life. Yes, my fourth Life Quadrant is part of the mix this year. Go, Davey, go. And, happy birthday, Buddy!

SO, WHAT DID I LEARN?

How did I make change EASYer on myself ☺ (or not ☹)?

In this chapter, you heard from Investment Portfolio Manager (a.k.a. Balanced Lifestyle Manager) Dave. I would be remiss if I didn't mention one of the greatest investment managers of our time, Warren Buffet. What would Warren Buffet have to share with us about making our balanced life portfolios EASYer on ourselves? If he ever reads this book, I'll certainly welcome his input but, in the meantime, I'm going to speculate.

For those of you who are not familiar with Warren Buffet, he is a value investor, so I'm confident that he would remind us to remember our values when choosing where to spend our time, both within each of and between our Life Quadrants. Not just where to spend it, but also with whom to spend it. Warren Buffet is also a big proponent of holding on to your investments for the long term. Earlier on we learned about the principle that "you are the average of the five people that you spend the most time with." If that's the case, and if, like Warren Buffet, you are a proponent of the longer-term approach, then you'll want to choose those people wisely. Once again, your values might come in handy.

Values! Follow the compass I referred to earlier. Maintain your balance by using your values GPS. I'm not sure how you can make your life journey any EASYer than that. I hope it's possible because that's exactly what I intend to do in the second half of my life. It took me a while to figure that one out, but better late, than never. ☺

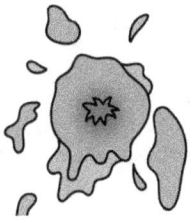

That was all about me. What about YOU?

What are you doing to make your journey of change EASYer on yourself? ☺ (or not ☹)?

How are you spending your time?

_____

_____

Are you aligned with your values?

_____

Are you showing up in all of your Life Quadrants the way you would like to?

_____

If not, what needs to change so you can do that?

_____

_____

If you are, what do you need to do in order to squeeze even more joy out of each quadrant?

_____

_____

When I'm old and dying, I plan to look back on my life and say "Wow, that was an adventure," and not, "Wow, I sure felt safe."
Tom Preston-Werner, Co-founder, Gifthub

PART 5
Captain Courageous
(2017-R.I.P.)

> # NEWer DAVE
> # 1965 - TBD
> ### He did his best to live every day to the fullest.
> ### JOY • FUN • PASSION • EXCITMENT
> ### No looking back. No Regrets.

Chapter 24:
The Start of My Second Half. Not quite.

If you want to make God laugh,
tell him your plans.

Unknown

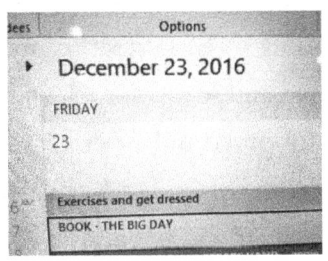

For someone who has a lot of ideas floating around his head, I can be quite organized at times. Really! A case in point is the picture of my calendar to the left. I actually scheduled the day I would finish writing this book; a date, that was also supposed to coincide with starting the second half of my life. I may have been a bit premature in my planning.

January 2, 2017. My Mini-Crash-and-Burn Learning Opportunity. Happy New Year. NOT!

According to my well-thought-out plans, one of my first priorities for the new year was to wrap up my book. My half-time was scheduled to finish on December 23, 2016 at 7:00 a.m. My second half was to start on January 1, 2017. I'm not sure what the week in between was for. Maybe a bit of a break.

A well-deserved break. It had been almost six years since I had started my half-time transition. Now that I had successfully transitioned from my half-time to the second half of my life, writing it all up in book format should not be that complicated, or so I thought.

Have you ever heard the expression, "If you want to make God laugh, tell him your plans"? Someone might have been laughing in early January (January 2) to be precise, when I realized, and rather quickly, that I had not yet transitioned. But it wasn't me. I wasn't laughing. In fact, I was a little disappointed at the time, and a little down on the emotional and energy fronts as well. It had been a while since I had felt down on those fronts, and I didn't like how it felt. For some reason, I had assumed that everything was going to be perfect in my second half. I was going to be happy and excited and ready to rock and roll, 24/7, 365 days of the year. Things were supposed to be perfect, a word I would later add to my "Avoid-the-Use-Of" word list. While I was at it, I would also add the word "assume" (and all its variations) to that list. I would also try my best not to make any assumptions as well, since they are rarely accurate.

But, back to early January. I was starting the year off with a bang on the work front. I was attending an annual event that I had really enjoyed in the past. I'd been looking forward to it for quite some time by then but, when the date finally rolled around, I didn't feel as excited as I had expected. I actually felt the opposite, I felt quite down. What was that? Was this not the beginning of my second half? My perfect second half? The negative feelings passed and my newly-developed positive, upbeat momentum came back in short order. But, I did decide that maybe I still had some work to do on myself, so finishing the book would have to wait. Apparently, I was still in my half-time transition. I had more to learn. Within a week, I was back up and running. Phew! I certainly didn't want to go back to where I had been before, during my dark days. There wasn't a whole lot of running back then, or any forward movement. I wasn't in a hurry to go back, but I also learned that I wasn't looking or striving for perfection, either.

"Life has its ups and downs but keep moving forward, Davey boy," I told myself, "because the downs will eventually pass." It was quite the learning experience. Let's see, what should I call this learning experience? How about my "mini-crash-and-burn" learning opportunity? That will differentiate it from the learning opportunity I was going to receive from a more profound crash-and-burn about six months later, what I refer to as my "Perfect Storm" opportunity, but more on that a little later (oh, great movie, by the way).

March 2017. Money. The Monkey on My Back. My New Freedom 55 Plan.

Ask people what scares them the most when it comes to making changes, especially ones on the career and business fronts, and you're sure to hear the "M" word come up, often. The "M" word being Money. Show me the money! You can add my name to that list. I'll admit it scares me, not always but, when it does, it can be very scary if I let it, and sometimes I do.

By this time in my transition as you'll read in the next chapter, Captain Courageous had pretty much dealt with many of my fears. There were no longer a lot of things that I was afraid to try; there weren't many things I was afraid to ask and/or share; and there weren't many people I was afraid to reach out to and connect with. But I still had one fear and that fear was money, or my potential lack thereof. Yes, the "M" word. Apparently, Captain Courageous still had some battles to fight, and at least one more dragon to slay – a big, nasty, fire-breathing beast.

Accountant Dave reminded me regularly that there were no pressing financial issues at the time. I could use my savings to fund my business. Ironically, the money I had saved for my Freedom 55 retirement fund (my retirement from life fund) could be used to help fund what was fast becoming my new Freedom 55 plan, a new plan that would allow me to enjoy life instead of hide from it. How ironic is that? Not to mention convenient. It takes an average of at least five years to build a sustainable business – another reminder from Accountant Dave. What a coincidence! I had started building my business at 50, so I had only about 3 years to go; hence, the opportunity to re-purpose the funds from the Freedom 55 plan. Well, that worked out well!

Accountant Dave also reminded me of the book my mom had shared with me more than 30 years earlier, *Do What You Love, the Money Will Follow*. "Do what you love, Davey, and the money will follow," he told me. "You have savings, regular and retirement-related. You're not planning to retire anytime soon, or ever, for that matter, so you can use them both. You can always find something else to supplement your income temporarily as you build your business, if needed. Stay in the moment. Take it day by day. Don't panic!"

I think it was the accountant in me that was reminding me of all those things, but it might have been my Inner Coach and my outer coach (her name is Shawna) or a combination of all three. Regardless, I listened to them. Most of the time, I did, and it made a big difference. I was able to focus on doing what I felt was the right thing, not the desperate thing. I thank my advisors for their advice and encouragement and I'll also give myself a pat on the back for listening to them. Most of the time. I also caught myself listening to my Inner Critic. Not often, but sometimes. So, no pat on the back there, but, hey, I'm only human. I had accomplished so much, so no kick in the butt either. "Give up, Dave," my Inner Critic would say. "You can't do it. Go back to being an employee before you squander your money and your time. No one wants to read your book. You're an accountant, not a coach. Your kids are going to think you're a failure. Is that how you want them to see you? A role model for failure?"

Although I didn't listen to my Inner Critic that often, I did listen to him every once in a while. It was likely to become more frequent until I had a financially sustainable business model in place (one of my Top Six dreams, my goals) that would provide the funds needed to run my business and my life the way I wanted, not the way my Inner Critic wanted me to run it.

You hear that, Captain Courageous? You still have a dragon to slay! You might want to keep your armour on (my growth mindset and positive attitude) and your weapons handy (my network, my skills and my life experiences), because this one is a pretty big, nasty beast and he breathes fire!

July 2017. The Perfect Storm. Time to Tweak My Expectations. PERFECTION? Not!

Remember my mini crash-and-burn learning opportunity at the beginning of the year? I had another one about six months later. It was both larger in scale and longer in duration. At one point, I thought it would overtake me, but it eventually passed, and I prevailed. Yay, Dave! The negative emotions and negative energy and negative thoughts passed, but the learnings stayed with me. There were a lot of them; after all, they were the result of a "Perfect Storm."

Picture this for a moment: I had been going through a period of change for close to seven years. It had been close to 18 months since I had given up regular paycheques to start my own business, which, by definition, takes time to get up and running. Money was flowing out at a fast pace and wasn't yet flowing in at the same rate – nowhere near the rate I would have liked. Focusing on writing my book was not generating cash. Vacation time was upon us and it was slowing my coaching practice to a crawl. There was more than a bit of stress for me on the business front.

It was summer, and the kids were home from school. I hadn't yet adapted to the new four-quadrant routine and having them around more often resulted in even less time to spend on my business. Add to that my now active fourth Life Quadrant (spending time with a beautiful woman) and I was in trouble. Don't get me wrong, I'm not complaining. It was just that the addition of more time with my kids (and I wasn't giving this up) to the time I wanted to spend with my sweetheart (not giving this up, either) was destabilizing the delicate balance I had achieved in my routine to that point. To top it off, it was a rainy, wet summer. My favourite season of the year was sucking big time.

I was stressed beyond belief on my work-life balance front. I was just starting to feel as if I were finally able to maintain my balance as I was walking the wire that was my life journey and, here I was, feeling as if I had fallen right off that wire. Forget balancing, I was falling! After all that work, I had fallen off the wire. I had also fallen off the wagon. I was cheating on the drinking and eating front as well. Not often, and never a booze buzz, but often enough to gain some weight for the first time in more than three years. What's with that?

It was around this time that I started to feel a little down again but, this time, it was lasting longer than before. My positive attitude and energy level were not returning as quickly as before. The longer it went on, the more worried I got. I stopped using my processes and tricks and routines and started doubting them instead. All of a sudden, I was building negative momentum. I even contemplated putting my book on hold for a while, but a challenge from my coach (in this case my outer coach, Shawna) put an end to my plans for that one. Ironically, I did the opposite. Instead of postponing my book, I shifted my focus to my book. If my business purpose was to inspire others to make positive changes in their lives, what better way to connect with as many people as possible than by finishing my book? Besides, it's summer. Everyone is off, and I can write by the pool, if ever the sun comes out. Okay, I get it, coach. Thanks for the encouragement. Now I just need the energy to pull it off.

Before I knew it, the energy was back. Some of the energy came back when I reminded myself of the progress I had made over the years. I was entitled to a bit of a summer break, and future breaks as well. Remember, resting is just as important as working. Note to self: Next time I schedule time off, not only will I stick to it, I will enjoy it as well. Some of my energy also came back when I decided to go back to what had helped me get to where I was in the first place – my tools and tricks, and processes and habits. I had taken my eye off them for what seemed like only a moment and my positive momentum had gone with it. Slowly, but surely, my momentum took a hit, or maybe it was my body forcing me to take a break. Or maybe there was so much change going on now that my fourth Life Quadrant was in gear, including a new set of extended relationships – Qita's family and friends, not to mention, her two beautiful daughters. Either way, when I decided to leverage my approach and tools, the momentum started to come back again, only this time, it seemed to come back even more quickly, and I was growing even faster. It was quite a good lesson to learn!

And it's a lesson that I'll use the next time I feel my emotions and energy slowing down. And it will happen. That's my other lesson learned. There will be ups and downs in the future and I'm going to fall off the tight rope again. I will fall but, more importantly, I will get up just as fast, if not faster. There are still going to be Mondays that suck! I am feeling pretty positive that they will be increasingly rare but I am not going to stress myself out trying to make them all great, all of the time. I don't believe that is achievable and I don't want to waste my energy trying. I think that I will take a pass on that approach, thank you very much. F**K PERFECTION.

Now, if you don't mind, I think that I'm finally ready to start my second half. I'll let you know how it goes in one of my next books, Maintaining It. Cheers!

SO, WHAT DID I LEARN?

How did I make change EASYer on myself ☺ (or not ☹)?

I was listening to the radio this morning. The radio hosts were talking about a concept around being happy. They were talking about the difference between being happy and being happy all the time. In my case, it was my desire to have fun, to have fun all the time, even on Mondays – every Monday, that had ended up stressing me out! Time to give up that quest for perfection. And here I was thinking I had abandoned that quest. ☹ Well, this is NEWer Dave and his new motto is to have fun, not all the time, but, at least, most of the time. Screw perfection. Although my desired state of being is having fun, I was going to cut myself some slack in order to make things EASYer on myself. ☺ I was going to have fun most of the time, but not all of the time. Bye-bye, stress. Bye-bye, perfection. Good riddance, I don't find either of you much fun! No matter what day of the week it is.

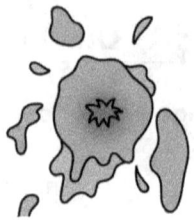

That was all about me. What about YOU?

What are you doing to make your journey of change EASYer on yourself? ☺ (or not ☹)?

Are you striving for perfection?

_____

If so, how is that quest treating you?

_____

_____

Is it time to cut yourself some slack?

_____

How might you take small steps toward your desired end goal, rather than massive ones that often have the potential for extra stress and getting stuck?

_____

_____

_____

_____

Chapter 25: Keeping My Courage

If you need someone to trust, trust yourself.

Bob Dylan

The above picture is of the stairs leading down to my mancave (a.k.a. cinema room). I am no Michelangelo but I got inspired one night with some paint and a brush. I must have been watching *Braveheart*.

August 2017. Captain Comfort Zone Has Left the Building but He Hasn't Gone Far.

It took him a while, but Captain Courageous finally showed up, and he seems to be sticking around these days. By a while, I mean it took him several years. It was a bit of an iterative process, really. I started developing my courage at work in my previous role; then, as I was launching my new business; next, as I was developing my relationships and improving my communication skills; and, finally, as I was reaching out in my quest to find my soulmate.

It took me a while because I needed to gain a certain level of confidence in myself and, for me, that could only come from collecting and processing evidence (i.e. trying things out). So, try I did – that is, Captain Courageous did – and the rest is history. I still like to provide Captain Courageous with a challenge every so often (e.g. I changed a car tire all by myself a couple of months ago, and I drove through the streets of Manhattan a couple of weeks ago) in order to keep him on his toes but, for the most part, I'm not feeling all that fearful these days. Unfortunately, though, Captain Comfort Zone is lurking in the vicinity. He might have left the building but he's hanging around the entrance waiting to sneak back in. It turns out that lack of courage is not the only thing that can keep me in my comfort zone.

Captain Comfort Zone has some other friends, a whole bunch of them. A bunch of shady characters. Captain Complacency is one of them. You may have heard of him. When push comes to shove, he's the one advocating for settling for less. Captain Procrastination goes by the motto, "Why do today what we can do tomorrow? (or the day after, or next week)? There's Captain Distraction. As far as he's concerned, the more distractions the merrier, since more, in this case, results in getting less done or, ideally, nothing done.

The above are only a few of the characters I have to contend with as I embark upon my second-half journey. And let's not forget my Inner Critic. I see him as the leader of the gang, encouraging one or more of the others to join him in what seems to be his mission to derail my life journey any way he can. And he often strikes when I'm least expecting it, or when I'm least prepared to fight him off, such as late at night or when I'm feeling a bit down. At least I'm aware of him and them and, remember, awareness is nine-tenths of the battle.

Although I know that Captain Comfort Zone and his cronies are around, they can be hard to spot. For example, it can be challenging to differentiate between procrastination and a need to take a break and recharge. I guess that's where getting to know myself and my limits comes into play. Not to mention my schedule; more specifically, my scheduled time off.

Ah, well, upwards and onwards, Davey boy. No one said your second half was going to be easy. The premise is that it will be EASYer and much, much more fulfilling but, be wary, there are always obstacles and nasty characters waiting to trip you up. You've come a long way, Captain Courageous, don't let those folks tell you otherwise. Kudos to you.

Fall 2017. Welcoming NEWer Dave to the Fold. And What Better Way than with a Little TLC!

Speaking of shady characters, one of the nastiest reared his ugly head recently. Now that I think of it, he has shown up on many occasions in the past, almost always accompanied by my Inner Critic. They make a formidable team. But this time, he seemed especially nasty. His name is Thomas, Doubting Thomas (or DT, for short). His area of expertise? Planting and sowing seeds of self-doubt, especially as they relate to dreams and aspirations.

When DT showed up, it was during my recent perfect storm. And what perfect storm would be complete without him? I'm not sure who invited him to the party, but he was there and doing his best to put as many doubts in my mind as possible. My belief in my dreams. My belief in myself. He didn't pick on any one belief, they were all fair game! "You're no author!" "Who's going to read your book?" And so on. I buckled but I did not break. It was easy to bend, lower my expectations and reel in my dreams. And, suddenly, my Comfort Zone was feeling comfortable again. I really struggled to come up with the energy and desire to keep writing. I almost started believing DT. But, fortunately for me, my faith in myself and my dreams were too strong for him. Not only did my inspiration for writing return during that relatively short period, I even came up with ideas for my next three books. Take that, DT! Can I put you down for a copy?

DT is gone now but I'm pretty sure he'll be back and, when he does, I'll be waiting for him. In the meantime, I have some things to attend to, including, apparently, writing a few more books.

Oh! A Little Bit of TLC along the Way Can Make all the Difference. A Little or a LOT. Here's What that Looks Like:

TRUST. What I have found is that, in addition to a bit of faith, a bit of trust can help out on that front as well. To trust myself. Yes, the "T" word. A word that makes Doubting Thomas cringe. Apparently, trust is not only important in developing and maintaining relationships, it's also important in developing and maintaining faith in my dreams and in myself. I might not be able to come up with evidence to support my dreams, since they haven't happened yet, but I can come up with evidence to support my trust in myself. How often had I become discouraged during my half-time transformation, only to pick myself up again shortly thereafter? How often did I deviate from my goals and plans only to re-orient myself? How often? Often! Very often!

Before I knew it, I felt like I had my own back. I started to trust myself, and the more I trusted myself, the EASYer it was to fall and not get discouraged. I knew I'd be back up on my feet moving forward again, either the next day, or the next week or, in the case of the perfect storm, the following month. I trusted myself. I trusted that I was doing the right thing and that I would continue to do so. It felt amazing! Go, Davey, Go!

LOVE. The "L" word. I had been a big fan of self-compassion for a while when I joined an ex-colleague and friend of mine for lunch a short time ago. She's the friend I mentioned earlier who had also undergone a significant transformation that involved a change in lifestyle, one that had also resulted in weight loss, among many other health benefits. She looked so healthy now, she was radiant.

As you can imagine, our discussion soon turned to exchanging tips and techniques on how we had both made and maintained our life changes. I mentioned that I had put together a preliminary list of my Top 10 Change Enablers, and one of my favourites was being compassionate toward myself. How often do people beat themselves up for doing something they thought they should not have done? Or, not doing something that they thought that they should have? Well, not me. I had eaten a cookie the other night and I did not scold myself. I had cheated and eaten one cookie. How compassionate of me.

"One cookie?" she replied. "I will sometimes go on an eating binge, junk food and dessert to boot. Do I feel guilty when I do? No. It is what it is. I will go back to heathier eating when I'm ready. I trust myself and have enough confidence and love for myself that there is no doubt or worry whatsoever." Wow. Self-love.

Note to self: Upgrade self-compassion to self-love on my Top 10 List.

CONFIDENCE. Courage isn't the only "C" word that comes to mind when I think of Captain Courageous. Confidence is another. Since they are related, I figure I can cheat and include them both.

When push comes to shove. When the unknown rears its ugly head. When things start to get scary, I can't think of anything more important than summoning the courage to just keep moving forward. Having the confidence that I'm moving in the right direction. Having the confidence that I will be courageous enough to keep moving forward regardless of the challenges. I won't be afraid in the face of the many fire-breathing dragons I encounter, for I will have my knight in shining armour next to me. I will have Captain Courageous right next to me. Welcome, Captain Courageous. Welcome, Captain Confidence. I'm looking forward to our journey together.

Trust, Love and Confidence. Put all three of those words together and what do you get "TLC." Aside from a little "tender loving care," I can't think of anything else that will serve me as well as I embark upon my journey, on my second-half life journey.

Enjoy the journey, NEWer Dave. The second half of your newer life journey! You, too, Captain Courageous.

And remember, I LOVE YOU, buddy!

SO, WHAT DID I LEARN?

How did I make change EASYer on myself ☺ (or not ☹)?

BELIEF in myself. I'm not sure I could maintain the energy to move forward along the path I believe is best for me without it. Yet I find that belief ebbs and flows and, when it ebbs, that's when I have to try to make it EASYer on myself by drawing on a little TLC. "T" is for Trust (as in myself). "L" for Love (of the unconditional kind). And, last but not least, "C" is for Confidence and Courage (in my case, one of my new-found friends).

And don't forget the other more well-known TLC, "Tender Loving Care." Remember to share some of it with others. It might just encourage them to share some back. ☺ Next thing you know, your TLC bucket will be overflowing from both the giving and receiving. That will come in handy during the times when your beliefs and energy levels are on the low side.

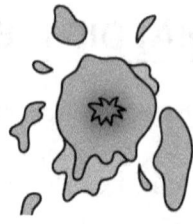

That was all about me. What about YOU?
What are you doing to make your journey of change EASYer on yourself? ☺ (or not ☹)?

What type of characters are hanging around with you these days?

_____

_____

Are they nasty or nice?

_____

_____

Can you start noticing when you're allowing the nasty ones to take charge…and then invite them to step down?

_____

_____

How can you show yourself more TLC?

_____

_____

In any given moment, we have two options. To step forward into growth or to step back into safety.
Abraham Maslow

PART 6
Thinking of Making a Change to Your Story?

Chapter 26: My Top Three Lessons Learned

*Change is hard at first, messy in
the middle and gorgeous at the end.*

Robin Sharma

Making Change as Easy as 1-2-3. Okay, Maybe Not Easy, but EASYer. My Top Three Take-Aways.

I have already shared my overarching strategy of making change EASYer by coming up with ways to make change EASYer on myself. Making change fun, if possible, also doesn't hurt. I will also share my Top 10 List of Change Enablers in the next chapter. But first, here are my Top Three Lessons Learned in making change EASYer on myself. I call it the "Power of Three." I am hoping that you can leverage these lessons to make change EASYer on YOU. Making and maintaining it. Farther and faster.

#1 - It Starts and Ends with You. It's Your Choice to Move forward or Not. You Are the Enabler.

In the end, YOU means YOU. The buck stops with YOU. I did it. I made the change. I had a lot of help and support from others – a lot of others, including my life coach, my relationship counselor, and my family and friends. I had help from too many others to thank them all in this book. You know who you are! You were all such an incredible support in helping me make all these changes in my life. You have had such a positive impact on my life. I will be forever grateful. Hopefully, I'll have the chance to pay it back and pay it forward. Thank you, all!

But, ultimately, I did it. The change enabler was ME, MYSELF and I. I was the one who got up every morning and did it. When push came to shove, I was the one who was pushed and the one who was shoved. When I fell down, I picked myself up. When I failed, I kept going. When I got stuck, I got unstuck. When there was something to learn, I learned it. When there was something to try, I tried it. And so on and so on. I'm not sure how I did it sometimes, but I did. I didn't have to do any of those things, but, ultimately, it was up to me. Not my coach, not my boss, not my relationship counselor, not my friends, not my family, not my soulmate. No, it was all me. The buck stopped with me.

And, if the buck stops with me when it comes to making change in my life, that means that the buck stops with YOU when it comes time to making change in YOUR life. If YOU want to undertake a change in your life, remember that you'll be the one making it. When things get tough, the tough get going, and the person who will need to get tough to get going, will be you. After all, no one can do it for you. When push comes to shove, what I discovered is that You Gotta Want It! When push comes to shove, you really gotta want it. It was when I really wanted to change that I finally started the process. It was that straightforward. I was no longer hoping to change. I no longer felt a need to change. I no longer felt a pressure to change. I wanted to change.

Whether the motivator for change is to end something painful or to start something joyful, it starts with wanting to do it. To really want to do it. If you don't want to do it, it won't take you long to come up with an excuse not to. I had tried to make changes before, especially when it came to living a healthy lifestyle. I felt the need, but I did not truly want to do it. I was pushing myself to do it, and, when push came to shove, I wasn't able to hang in there. Despite my best intentions, the new treadmill would become the dusty treadmill and one of many pieces of exercise equipment gathering dust in my house until the next garage sale came around.

In hindsight, I am glad I didn't sell the treadmill. It has served me well over the past year as part of my early morning wake-up routine. I actually took a walk on it earlier this morning. I enjoy the exercise and the reading I get done while on it. It's a great way to start the day, so I often start my day on my treadmill, not because I have to, but because I want to.

#2 - It Takes Time and Effort. One Step at a Time. Just Start. Just Give It a Try.

Looking to make an impactful change in your life? What I have found is that, if and when you do decide to go for it (i.e. you actually decide to start), it takes time. One step at a time. One Life Quadrant at a time. One day at a time, and sometimes, when the going is really rough, one minute at a time. There is no magic six-week "Change Your Life" workshop out there, despite what people might tell you.

Just starting is how you start your journey. It is that easy! Keeping at it, in order to finish your journey, is where it gets a little tougher, and takes much longer. Without the foundation to support your growth, you will eventually stumble and fall, and foundations take time to build. That's where making it EASYer on yourself really comes into play. Oh and, enjoying the ride makes it, so much EASYer!

When I look back to the beginnings of my self-transformation, the thing I find the most surprising is just how much I had changed before I really noticed that I had changed. When I finally decided to change, I made it so easy on myself to change, and I was actually having so much fun, and enjoying myself, that I didn't realize I was changing. I hadn't set out to do many of the things that I ended up doing. I had no specific weight-loss goals but, before I knew it, my pants were falling off and I was investing in a new wardrobe. Before I knew it, I was not only eating healthy, but enjoying it and, next thing I knew, the food in my fridge and cupboards had completely changed – and changed to be healthier, I might add.

Some people make it so hard on themselves to change from the get-go that they're not able to get far at all. Some people make it so hard on themselves that they don't even want to start and, so, they don't. But here I was, doing my best to make it EASYer on myself and have fun, and it seems to have worked, at least for me. I will leave the "making it HARDer on yourself" approach to others, thank you very much! Good thing I decided to take the "make it EASYer on myself" approach because, as it turned out, my transformation was a long one. It was long, and it was a lot of work. Change implies that something will become different and, if there's no movement, how can something become different? How can I change something if nothing happens, if there is no action or movement? How can I change if I do nothing?

I just kept moving. I just kept changing. I persevered. I learned by failing and I learned by succeeding; in my case, I kept at it for close to seven years.

And, despite my attempts to make everything EASYer on myself, there were times, many times, when it got so tough that the only thing I could do was to take one step at a time. Even just one step was hard on those occasions. There were times when my motivators, my dreams, and my passion were not enough to keep me going. It was as if they had disappeared. At those times, I just had to keep at it and that meant I had to keep moving. One step at a time.

#3 - Don't Go It Alone.

Going it alone. Trying to live life in isolation. Hiding out. Trying to make change alone. Been there, done that and it doesn't work, at least, not for long. As mentioned, I have a saying taped to the wall in my office. It says, "If you want to go fast, go alone. If you want to go far, go together." A bit of a reminder that isolating myself, especially when things aren't going well, is not exactly a best practice in making change EASYer on myself.

As I mentioned, making a change in your life implies doing something differently. So, doesn't it make sense to expand your lens on life by connecting with others? Doesn't it make sense to gain a better understanding of yourself by seeing yourself through the lenses of others? Remember the story of how I had become someone I was not? It was someone else who pointed that out to me. I had my blinders on. I was in full-steam-ahead mode. I stopped for nothing and no one. Unfortunately, I was not heading in the right direction. Fortunately, someone else had the courage to call me on it, and I had the good sense to stop and listen to them.

When you fall, and you will, isn't it comforting to know someone is nearby to help you up? And, if not actually pick you up, at least help you gain, or regain, the energy to pick yourself up? When it comes to choosing people who will play a big part in your life, remember the saying "misery likes company" and choose wisely.

And what about those times when you're moving so fast you don't notice that, maybe, just maybe, it's time to take a bit of a break and recharge? If you're not self-aware, and despite our best attempts, sometimes we're not, isn't it comforting to know that someone else is there? Someone who isn't afraid to call you out on something even if that means maybe hurting your feelings.

Remember what I learned in my coaching school, my life coaching school: "People grow from connection. Connection is the wellspring of creativity. Collaboration is the conduit for enhancing people's strengths."[44] Amazing! Connecting with others enhances our ability to play to our strengths. What a great idea! You would have thought that my Ideation strength would have picked up on that one earlier on. Oh, well, better late than never. In this case, just in time for the next phase of my life journey, the second half of my life!

SO, WHAT DID I LEARN?

How did I make change EASYer on myself ☺ (or not ☹)?

There is one thing that stands out amidst all I have accomplished during this seven-year period of change (and counting!). For each and every change, I started by just starting. As a colleague of mine, Hugh Culver, recently pointed out in one of his blogs, the secret to making a change is to just start.[45] One small step at a time. Every time now, when I become daunted by the perceived magnitude of making a new change, I make it EASYer on myself by just getting started. Just one thing. One small step. One small step at a time. Before I know it, I end up somewhere I would never have believed possible!

Oh! And don't forget to take care of yourself. Grab the oxygen mask if and when it comes down. Remember that change takes time. Make it EASYer on yourself by taking care of yourself. And by taking care of yourself, a little bit of self-compassion and self-love goes a long way. And a lot of self-compassion and self-love goes and gets you even farther. ☺

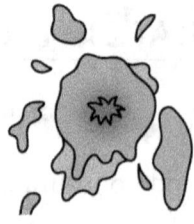

That was all about me. What about YOU?

What are you doing to make your journey of change EASYer on yourself? ☺ (or not ☹)?

Do you want to make a change...and make it stick?

_____

_____

Who is stopping you? Hopefully not you!

_____

_____

What is the first step you can take today to start building your momentum?

_____

_____

What's one thing you can do today to help you become more of the person you would like to be in life?

_____

_____

Chapter 27: My Top 10 Change Enablers

The sooner you step away from your comfort zone, the sooner you'll realize that it really wasn't all that comfortable.

Eddie Harris Jr.

I refer to the photo at the beginning of this chapter as my "before and after collage". It helps convey just how much change I have undergone over the past few years. People no longer recognize me. On the downside though, all of these pictures only capture part of my story. My transformation, from OLD Dave (on the left) to NEWer Dave (on the right), covered so much more than what can be seen on the outside. Unfortunately, I don't have photos of my insides. There are no "before" photos of my heart when it was three sizes too small, no "after" photos to show how much it has grown. There are no photos of my brain showing the neural pathways relating to my increasing emotional connections. You'll just have to trust me when I say that there's been as much change on the inside as on the outside.

I'm Sharing My Top 10 List of Change Enablers in the Hope You Will Add One or More to Yours!

The courage to finally leave my "comfort home" and trade in my "Captain Comfort Zone" cape for my "Captain Courageous" cape was enabled by a whole bunch of things that affected me on both the outside and the inside. I tried a whole lot of things. Some stuck and some did not. As previously mentioned, I did not come up with anything new. I basically begged, borrowed and stole what worked for others as a starting point in order to find out what worked for me. Hopefully I have conveyed that message to you earlier in this book. In this chapter, I have done my best to reduce all those enablers to my favorite kind of list, a Top 10 List. In this case, a Top 10 List of Change Enablers that were the most helpful to me, the unique me, in my unique situation. I hope that some, if not all, of these Change Enablers will work for YOU, too. The unique you, in your unique situation.

Oh, and by the way, I have found that, not only do these change enablers help enable change and transformation, they also help maintain those changes and transformations. As previously mentioned, that is often hard to do. Hopefully these will make it EASYer on you. I guess we could also call them Change Maintainers. Another double tap. Two for the price of one. Feel free to beg, borrow and steal to your heart's content. To your body's content. To your mind's content. To your soul's content.

CHANGE ENABLER #1
Maintain your mindset. A positive one!

(A positive attitude and a growth mindset. The choice is yours!)

I am convinced that life is 10% what happens to me and 90% how I react to it. And so it is with you... we are in charge of our attitudes.

Extract from the poem *"Attitude"* Charles Swindoll

Attitude. Mindset. And, while we are at it, let's throw in Momentum. The choice and consequences are yours and, by association, the resulting consequences of that choice are yours. Choose wisely. In coaching they remind us that everyone has a choice. I believe that now. When it comes to choosing between a positive and a negative attitude, the choice and resulting consequences are yours. When it comes to choosing between a growth mindset and a fixed mindset, the choice and resulting consequences are yours. When it comes to creating momentum, you can choose to move forward or backward or remain static. The choice and consequences are yours. And in the case of momentum, the consequence is that your choices will take you in the direction you choose, whether positive or negative, faster than you might think possible. So, as mentioned, and it's worth repeating, choose your direction wisely.

CHANGE ENABLER #2
Connect with the unique you. Often!

(Self-awareness. Get to know yourself better!
The real and authentic you!)

WHO ARE YOU? Who, who? Who, who?

Lyrics from the hit song "*Who are you?*" THE WHO

Making it EASYer on yourself starts with getting to know yourself better. Really getting to know yourself (the term we use in coaching is self-discovery). Your hopes, your dreams, your values, your strengths, your preferences, etc. They become your GPS and roadmap and tool kit as you embark upon and shape your journey of change. Deviate too much from your path and your GPS will alert you. Ignore it at your peril. It might suggest another route for getting back on track but it's up to you to take it. It might just hint that you are deviating from a more optimal route without actually telling you what that route is. And by YOU, I mean the real and authentic you. Your GPS, not someone else's.

CHANGE ENABLER #3
Connect with others. The right others!

(Remember, you are the average of the
five people you hang around with the most)

People grow from connection.
Principle #4 - Coach U Nine Guiding Principles of Human Interaction[46]

Expand your lens and expand your world of possibility. I could write another book on all the great ideas and insights and lessons learned that I've been exposed to by connecting with others over the past couple of years. I could write yet another book on all that I have discovered about myself by connecting with those same kind and caring others. Positive and encouraging others. They say, "misery loves company." What I discovered was that "positivity also likes company." That was the company I wanted to keep, the positive and motivating kind. Not only did my lens expand and open up a whole new world of ideas I would never have considered on my own, but it also allowed me to get to know myself better. I expanded my own lens on who I am by connecting with others. How cool is that?

Change Enabler #4
Just get going! Today, not tomorrow!

(Just try it. Just do it. But do it your way!
Fail at it. Learn from it. But keep moving forward.)

FAIL = First Attempt In Learning

Time to start moving. You're starting to get to know yourself better. Your lens and your corresponding world of possibilities are starting to expand by connecting with others and yourself. By possibilities, I mean the theoretical kind. It's time to make the theory real by experiencing it. By feeling it. It's time to "walk the talk." Time to learn. Time to grow. F**k next steps. More like, what is the next step. It can be one step forward and two steps back at first, as long as there is some momentum. Momentum leads to learning. Learning leads to growing. Growing leads to changing. Changing leads to shifting. Shifting leads to transforming. Transforming leads to maintaining and sustaining. So, it's time to ask your inner critic to take a back seat. You and your inner coach have some exploring to do. Remember, when YOU start to walk the talk, actions and change start to take place. So, put your seat belt on. When the momentum kicks in, you're in for quite the ride. Enjoy!

Change Enabler #5
Don't give up. Call on your GRIT!

(Call on your Passion and your power to Persevere.)

Grit: Perseverance and passion for long-term goals. Now recognized as one of the key determinations of success and life satisfaction.[47]

The two "C" words, Confidence and Courage, take time and effort to develop, and they take more time and effort to maintain. So, a little of the "P" word, Perseverance, will help. Actually, a lot of perseverance. And, Discipline. Until you can make your desired state a habit, discipline and perseverance will become your best friends. Remember to thank them with an occasional word of acknowledgement and a pat on the back. And, by occasionally, I actually mean often, very often. Celebrate your accomplishments. Celebrate your learnings. Celebrate your failures. Celebrate them by yourself and with others. And when it comes to summoning and maintaining the discipline and strength to persevere, it doesn't hurt to be passionate about what it is that you're trying to accomplish in the first place. What I found was that there was a pretty strong correlation between the score on my passion meter and my ability to summon the energy and courage to persevere. Passion + Perseverance = GRIT. The accountant in me likes that equation.

Change Enabler #6:
Manage your energy level. Wisely!

(Energize yourself. Often! And that might mean taking it EASYer on yourself more often!)

I have the power to manage the energy plant that is my body."

A quote from a dear friend who has helped me more than she knows in enabling my transition of transformation.

If self-awareness is truly nine-tenths of the journey, then it would stand to reason that the sooner we become aware of what giveth us energy and what taketh it away, the better. Not just the WHAT, the WHEN and the WHERE, but also the WHO. Do the people you spend time with add to or diminish your energy? Inquiring minds want to know! And, don't forget, it's your energy. Only you have control over it. As my dear friend put it when describing some of the magic she harnessed in making and maintaining her recent life-altering transformation, "I came to the realization that I have the power to manage the energy plant that is my body. My body. My energy plant. A plant that can produce energy and I have total control over mine." Wow! That was a life-altering idea! So, although I'm generally not a big fan of advice, especially of the unsolicited kind, I'll offer, let's call it, a suggestion: use your energy wisely, on the activity, timing, location, tools and especially people sides of the equation.

Change Enabler #7:
Take good care of your foundation. Regularly!

(Both your personal and your professional foundation.)

Rome wasn't built in a day.

I am an accountant, not an architect or engineer, but if there's one thing my change journey has taught me over the past few years, it's the importance of the strength and resilience of my personal and professional foundation. The foundation that supports all the learning and growth that change entails is not only important, it is a key enabler of change. In my haste and excitement to change, I crashed and burned more than once. If you don't believe me, I can show you the scars. They are fading now, and they weren't that bad, but I did get a few scrapes and bruises. And don't forget that "personal" means you. That's right, your personal foundation is all about you, what supports you. Change requires work. Work on your foundation, which means work on you.

It doesn't have to be hard work. You can make it EASYer on yourself. It can be fun as well. Again, it's totally up to you. But it does mean work. So, if you'd like to make some positive changes in your life but don't quite have the time – there are so many commitments and so little time with the career, the kids, the dog, the lawn, the cottage, (insert your excuse here) – you might want to try again later when you have more time.

But for those of you who are willing to make the time, remember this: although it's your foundation, you don't have to go it alone. Grab some tools. Ones that work for you. Come up with a strategy and/or approach and/or supporting processes and/or supporting protocols.

Again, ones that work best for YOU. Partner with others. Out-source stuff. In-source stuff. Do fewer things. Do more of the right things. Whatever it takes for you. Whatever works for you to build, maintain and expand the foundation to support you on your journey. In my humble opinion, there's nothing like a strong foundation to provide the strength, resilience, confidence and courage to reach for our dreams. To live our dreams. Whatever those dreams may be.

CHANGE ENABLER #8
Love yourself. 24/7!

(Love yourself. Yes, the "L" word.
Don't be afraid to use it on yourself as well as on others.)

I LOVE YOU, buddy! David Arthur Walker

Screw self-care. We're talking about some serious life-altering, self-transformational change here. Time to bring out the big guns. The "L" word. Love. Self-love. That doesn't mean that you stop loving others. Just the opposite. What I've found is that the more loving I was with myself, the more loving I felt toward others. Pretty soon I was throwing around the "L" word, a word I rarely used in the past, like it was the hottest buzz word out there. For me, it was. My love bucket started to runneth over and, wow, that came in handy on those days when I wasn't having fun and my energy was down. And, when my energy was down, guess what else would come down? My oxygen mask. I would grab it. Using it had served me well in the past. I was confident it would serve me well in the here and now. And guess what else? In the oxygen mixture, there was a nice little dose of self-love. I'm not sure how and when that got mixed in, but I'm grateful it was. It took me more than 50 years, but better late than never. I love you, buddy!

CHANGE ENABLER #9
Trust in yourself. Unwaveringly!

(When belief in yourself gets tough, trust in yourself comes in handy.)

If you can trust yourself when all men doubt you but make allowance for their doubting too.

Extract from the poem "IF" by Rudyard Kipling.
(BTW, I am assuming this applies to women as well.)

To believe in your dreams, to believe in your vision for your life, to believe in yourself — to truly believe — takes a lot of time. It takes a lot of evidence. It takes a lot of grit. There are a lot of questions to answer. Many of the "why" variety. I can't tell you how many times I felt convinced that I believed in what I was doing, only to wake up late in the night in a cold sweat worrying about the journey I was on and doubting myself and my abilities to get there. It took time to make that shift, the mind shift, to become a true believer. And even the true believer in me has days, and nights, when I have doubts. At first, I felt I had let myself down whenever I felt like I had become, what I call, a non-believer. But I realize now that this is a normal part of the journey. There will be lots of change and ups and downs along the way and many unknowns and some will be scary. As previously mentioned, the only constant is change. Although these days, I feel as if there is another constant in my life and that is the trust that I have developed in myself. I have truly become my own best friend. I feel as if I have my own back, not only every once in a while, but always. So, when the going gets tough and I lose a bit of faith in my beliefs, and, yes, get scared, it is my trust in myself that I have my own best interests in mind that keeps me moving forward. So, here is a toast to trust, because in the end, trust trumps doubt and fear, and that is enough to make a believer out of me.

CHANGE ENABLER #10
Remember who's in the driver's seat. YOU!

(You are holding the steering wheel.
Which direction do you want to go?)

*If you think you can or think you can't.
You are right.*

Henry Ford

This is your life, not someone else's. You are unique. Your situation is unique. No one knows you better than you. No one knows your dreams and your capabilities better than you. No one knows your situation like you. No one understands the background and context for your desired change better than you. Who will explore more opportunities and strategies to make that change happen for you? Who is better at making choices for you than you? So, who better to be in the driver's seat than you? Like it or not, you are driving. You set the pace and you set the direction. Challenges and input can be welcomed or ignored, but the decisions and direction are ultimately up to you. You can keep moving forward and live the life of your dreams, or you can remain in neutral and let life pass you by. Your choice. I suggest the former. That's the path I chose, and I haven't looked in the rear-view mirror since.

SO, WHAT DID I LEARN?

How did I make change EASYer on myself 😊 (or not ☹)?

Change is a process. It takes time and effort. There are no shortcuts. The Top 10 Enablers are just that, enablers. They need to be used in order to enable change and to maintain it. That takes time and that takes effort. It's a marathon, not a sprint. Adding time-outs every once in a while to recharge, reflect and reenergize yourself during the change process just might make your journey EASYer!

Oh, and taking a little time out to be grateful also goes a long way. Make a habit out of it. That's what I'm trying to do. Every morning when I wake up, the first thing I try to remember to do is to think of all of the amazing things and people I'm so grateful to have in my life, including me. I am grateful to myself for having the courage to continue to make positive changes in my life. I'm grateful for the many loving and caring people in my life who are changing along with me. I'm grateful for both. There are so many positive things going on in my life, so many positive activities and people these days, that I feel spoiled. 😊 Quite the change from where I was in the past. Almost completely opposite to it. I have pulled a Costanza on my life! So, thank you, Dave, for finally deciding to make that life-altering, self-transformation. And thank you, everyone else, for helping me pull it off, helping me make that journey EASYer on myself. Thank you for being there for me. I am so grateful.

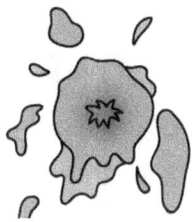

That was all about me. What about YOU?

What are you doing to make your journey of change EASYer on Yourself? ☺ (or not ☹)?

What key change enabler(s) are at the top of YOUR list?

_____

_____

_____

_____

What are you grateful for?

_____

_____

_____

Who are you grateful to have accompanying you on your journey?

_____

_____

_____

What is your next step in enabling your change?

_____

_____

_____

Can you do that right now? Or, if not, sometime today?

_____

_____

_____

If not, what's stopping you? What can you do to overcome that impediment?

_____

_____

_____

*Making a big life change is pretty scary.
But, know what's even scarier? Regret.*
Zig Ziglar

PART 7
Out with the Old and In with the NEWer You!

Chapter 28: WHO do you see in the mirror?

In the end, it's not the years in your life that count. It's the life in your years.

Abraham Lincoln

I thought it only fitting to include an image of a mirror here. After all, looking at myself in a mirror was one of my greatest catalysts for a change that was to become a self-transformation. I could have included the photo of my reflection in my mirror, but that would make it my mirror alone. And since this chapter is not about me, but about you, I have included a generic picture of a mirror as a placeholder, until you find the time, and the right timing, to take a peek into yours!

Take a Look in the Mirror and What Do You See? How Do You Feel? Is It Time to Make a Change?

Well, that was my story. What's yours? When you get up in the morning and look in the mirror, who's looking back at you? Is that you? More importantly, is that WHO you want to be? Forget the mirror for a second. How do you feel when you get up in the morning? Are you excited to start your day? Or, are you already looking forward to the end? Or, are you somewhere in between? Does it make a difference what day of the week it is? A weekday versus a weekend day? Monday versus Friday? Does it make a difference if you're at work? Or rest? Or play? Where are you in the life you want to lead? Are you considering making a bit of a change? Are you considering, maybe, making more of a change?

If you're considering making a change, are you ready and willing to take one on? If so, you'll want to be ready because change takes time and effort. Change requires a desire to make it happen. Going in kicking and screaming is not the way to go.

Want to Make a Change? What Are You Waiting for? Just Do It! Just Try It! Just Start!

I like to end my blogs with a challenge to my readers, so I decided to carry that tradition into this book. Here is my challenge to you. By you, I mean YOU. The person you see in your mirror. The person whose feelings you feel. [Insert your name here.] Yes, YOU! Are you ready for a change? A big one? A small one? Or, one in-between?

What I've found is that they all start the same way. One step at a time. One next step at a time. So, here's my challenge to you.

- Think of one change you want to make in your life.
- Think of the outcome you would like to achieve with that change.
- Think of how you will feel once you have made the change.
- Now, think of the next step in making that change happen.
- Not the next steps, just the next step. ONE next step.
- Then, do it. Just try it. Just start. What do you have you to lose?

Repeat the above as often as required. The more often, the merrier, but it all starts with that first step forward. That first step forward in a direction you want your life journey to take. And bonus points to you if you can make it EASYer on yourself, and, of course, have fun while doing it. You might even want to add another step to the process. Maybe add another question, i.e. "What is the best way to make this next step EASYer on myself?"

Whether your journey of change is a short one or a long one, no matter what path you follow, remember this: it doesn't have to be painful. There will be some tough times, but they need not be the rule, but rather the exception. It can be fun the majority of the time. A lot of fun. What better way can there be to make a change? I know because I did it. I made the change, and I had fun while doing it, and I plan on continuing to do so, as I continue through the second half of my life journey.

Just Do It. Or, Just Do the Opposite. Just Pull a Costanza!

If the only constant in life is change then, at some point in your life, at many points, you really won't have much of a choice but to change. That could involve making a change for the better or for the worse. Yes, you heard me right. If you would like to live a more joyful and fulfilling life or, if you would like to live a more miserable life, the process is the same.

When people ask me what I do in life, I often respond by saying "I help people make positive changes in their lives." I could just as easily say "I help people make negative changes in their lives." It's the same process, but I have yet to get any requests for help on becoming more miserable. I guess people are doing a good enough job for themselves on that score. The change process for good and bad is the same, but my hypothesis is that the way we go about inspiring ourselves to make changes can differ. The way we go about learning things about making change can differ. After all, we're all different. Just as some people learn more from a horror story (I count myself among them) than from a success story, some people are more receptive to ideas when communicated in a negative, rather than a positive way. Let's use one of my favorite books as an example.

The book is entitled *How to Be Miserable*, by Randy J. Paterson, PhD. If people out there are looking for help on "how to lead a more miserable life," you might want to add this to your reading list. It contains 40 strategies that, as the author puts it, "you already use."[48] You don't even have to start something from scratch. How cool is that? Or, uncool in this case, since the end-state is being more miserable. I read that book and found that the author did a great job of summarizing a lot of the change ideas I was reading about in my other books (and I read a lot of them!). All of my other self-help books, self-help of the positive kind, shared ideas on how to lead a happier, more joyful, more fulfilling, more [insert your positive life goal here] life. It was as if his 40 strategies covered all those ideas except that all of his ideas were on how to lead a more miserable life. If I want to make a positive change in my life, I have to read a hundred books but, if I want to make a negative change, I only have to read one. What's with that?

Well, I got to thinking. What if I picked one strategy that resonated with me; in my case, something I wanted to do less of, rather than more of, since I was trying to lead a more fulfilling and less miserable life. Instead of following the strategy laid out in the book, I would pull a Costanza and do the opposite. I would "just do it" but I would "just do the opposite." Just doing the opposite had served me well before, so what was stopping me from not leveraging that approach again?

This was a great way to continue to make more positive changes in my life, not to mention maintain the ones that I had already made! I think (I'll give that a try. Here's a good one from Paterson's book: "Lesson 21. Become an Island unto Yourself."[49] I've done that before, so it should be a lot EASYer to do the opposite now. And, by the way, I don't think that Randy would have any issues with me or YOU doing the opposite of any of the 40 strategies he shares, since he himself suggests just such an approach in his book.[50]

SO, WHAT DID I LEARN?

How did I make change EASYer on myself ☺ (or not ☹)?

I learned a lot during this period of transition of mine. More than during any other time in my life. Looking back now, if there is one thing that really stands out for me, it is that I like to share. I really, really like to share. I like to share because I care. I actually have separate folders in my email for all of my clients and key contacts where I archive the ideas and tools that I share. I name the folders "sharing and caring". I have hundreds of them. That love of sharing, I guess, is what has given me the strength and courage to share my story via this book. To share some pretty personal things, including my emotions. Yes, emotions, and I am a guy. Maybe that is another key lesson learned. That it is okay to share my emotions even if I am a guy.

There are a lot of people out there who are not where they want to be. Some are not sure where they want to be. They just know that they are not living the life that they want to be living. Others have an idea of where they want to go but are not able to get going. I hope that by sharing my story, I have helped some of them, and hopefully you. Not just to set out, which is hard enough, but to continue along that journey, even when times get tough. I hope that some of what I have shared has and will continue to make your Life Journey EASYer on you. Nothing would please me more!

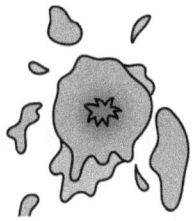

That was all about me. What about YOU?
What are you doing to make your journey of change EASYer on yourself? ☺ (or not ☹)?

Are you ready to get going? Are you ready to take that first next step in making a truly important change in your life? To start today! and not tomorrow. If so, hopefully I have provided enough ideas and tools (and some inspiration ☺) in this book to support the unique you through your unique journey of change. As a bonus, I have also included a number of additional tools and ideas in the resources section of this book, again, as a way of making change EASYer on you. In both enabling it and maintaining it.

Enjoy your journey of change! Here's wishing that it becomes a journey of transformation of the most positive and rewarding kind. You deserve it! Go get it! What are you waiting for?

Resources

The following is a Top 10 list of some of the "Who Are You" dimensions that you can further explore and leverage in helping you make and maintain positive changes in your life.

More details and related tools and resources for each of them can be accessed in my blog: "WHO are YOU? The Unique YOU! The Authentic YOU! How well Do YOU know YOU? Sharing MY Top 10 Ways that I got to know Myself Better."

Get the workbook blog at davewcoachingandstorytelling.com

Try one, try many, try them all. Put together your own "Who Are You" workbook!

1. Finding Your Primary Love Language (and enjoying it.)
2. Finding Your Personality a.k.a. Your Preferences (and embracing them.)
3. Finding Your Strengths (and playing to them.)
4. Finding Your Values (and honouring them.)
5. Finding Your EQ a.k.a. Emotional Intelligence (and applying it.)
6. Finding Your Vocation (and loving it.)
7. Finding Your Calling (and being purposeful about it.)
8. Finding Your Dreams (and believing in them and in You.)
9. Finding out how others perceive You a.k.a. Your Brand (and marketing to it.)
10. Finding Your Style. Your Leadership Style (and engaging others with it.)

BONUS: Finding Your Communication Style (and connecting with it.)

A Blog or Two to Help You Along Your Way!

I have expanded on many of the concepts in this book in my blogs. Here are few blogs that might prove helpful to you:

The Blog Name (i.e. Topic)	Helping You ...
Dave's Top 5 List: My Dream Job	Come up with or refine criteria to help you in choosing the right career opportunities for you.
Dave's Top 5 List: How I Lost Close to 100 Pounds of Body Fat	Make and maintain some changes on the living a healthier (and longer) life front.
Dave's Top 5 List: Traits of a Great Leader (as viewed through my lens)	Engage others using the key traits of a leader (as viewed through your lens).
Dave's Top 5 List: Top 5 10 Traits of MY Soulmate	Solidify your bond with your romantic partner and enjoy the results. Together!
Stress. Stress. Go Away!	Manage that nasty word, stress!
Our Next Generation of Leaders	Create some more of them while becoming a better one at the same time.
Let's Talk about My Bout with Clinical Depression	Become more aware of depression and the nasty effects that it can have on ourselves and those around us.
Are you playing to your strengths? MY top 10 learnings from playing to them with a bunch of 10-year-olds!	Further identify and leverage your strengths and those of the people around you. Ten-year-olds and older.
WHO are YOU? The Unique YOU! The Authentic YOU! How well Do YOU know YOU? Sharing MY Top 10 Ways that I got to know Myself Better	Better understand what makes you the unique you! And better still, how to play to your unique you!
Eating Healthy Does not have to Taste like S**T!	Eat nutritiously and feel better (without having to hold your nose while doing it).
How to Lead a Miserable Life or NOT.	Choose from 40 strategies to lead a more miserable life, or not, by doing the polar opposite of those strategies.
Yo! Leaders! Are you a Multiplier? or, a Diminisher?	Identify the extent that you are having a positive vs. a negative impact on the level of engagement of the people who are looking to you for leadership.
What is your Love language? Oh, and, Happy Valentines Day!	Nurture your love language and those of the ones that you love.
Have you updated your balance sheet lately?	Catalogue all of the skills and experiences and connections that you have going for you.

All of my previous blogs can be found in the blog section of my website at http://davewcoachingandstorytelling.com/blog/

While there, you can also register to receive newly published ones as I share them - hot off the virtual press! ☺

The Top 10 Change Enablers: One Page Self-Assessment

If the only constant in life is change, this little tool will help you monitor and manage your progress along the path of your life journey. Enjoy your journey!

Change Enablers (Chapter 27)	How am I doing? (Scale of 1-10)	What can I do differently? i.e. Start. Stop. Continue.
1. Maintain your mindset. A positive one!		
2. Connect with the unique you. Often!		
3. Connect with the right others. Often!		
4. Just get going. Today, not tomorrow!		
5. Don't give up! Call on your GRIT!		
6. Manage your energy level. Wisely!		
7. Take good care of your foundation. Regularly!		
8. Love yourself. 24/7!		
9. Trust in yourself. Unwaveringly!		
10. Remember who's in the driver's seat. YOU!		

Food for thought: In keeping with Change Enabler #2, "Connect with the unique you. Often!" you might want to consider taking this self-assessment more often than not. Remember self-awareness is nine-tenths of the battle (a.k.a. enabling the change along your life journey).

WARNING! Striving for perfection (i.e. a score of 10 across all 10 enablers all of the time) could lead to just a bit of stress, or lots of it. ☹ *If you have your heart set on a perfect 10, then may I suggest Change Enabler #8, "Love Yourself". I can't think of any situation in which one would not want to do so.*

Help Along Your Journey of Transformation

Helping YOU GO farther, faster by making Change EASYer on yourself

Life Coaching

My coaching offerings, individual and group, are part of my "virtual" global practice serving clients worldwide through Video or Voice only (whatever YOU feel most comfortable with).

1-to-1 Coaching (a.k.a. Individual Coaching)

There is no doubt in my mind that I have gone farther and faster in making and maintaining positive changes in my life as a result of the support and encouragement of my Life Coach.

If you would like to discuss how coaching can help you in enabling an important change and eventual transformation in your life. Reach out and let's see how, together, we can make that change EASYer on you!

Group Coaching

What better way to expand one's lens while exploring a journey of change than connecting with others who are also undergoing a similar journey.

I periodically offer group coaching sessions that are designed to help my clients gain a better understanding of themselves and the best path forward, for them, the unique them.

Here are a few examples of offerings:

- The "Who Are You?" Virtual Group Coaching Experience
- The Authentic Leadership Bootcamp
- Connect with your communication style but don't forget your blind spots

For More Details

Feel free to take a peek at my website for more information on any of my Coaching offerings. www.davewcoachingandstorytelling.com

Endnotes

1. Songwriters: Mark David Hollis/Timothy Alan Friese-Greene. Life's What You Make It lyrics © Universal Music Publishing Group.
2. Inspired by Finding Joe, a film by Patrick Takaya Solomon (2011).
3. Marsha Sinetar, Do What You Love, the Money Will Follow (Dell, 1989).
4. Bob Buford, Halftime: Moving from Success to Significance (Zondervan, 2015).
5. <http://davewcoachingandstorytelling.com/2016/09/01/blog-04/> (1 September 2016).
6. Inspired by the book, How Full is Your Bucket?, by Tom Rath and Donald O. Clifton (Gallup Press, 2004).
7. <https://www.linda-ellis.com/the-dash-the-dash-poem-by-linda-ellis-.html>.
8. Buford, p. 73.
9. <www.davewcoachingandstorytelling.com>.
10. Don Miguel Ruiz, The Four Agreements (Amber-Allen Publishing, 1997).
11. http://davewcoachingandstorytelling.com/2017/03/03/have-you-updated-your-balance-sheet-lately/ (3 March 2017).
12. Dan Kindlon and Michael Thompson, Raising Cain: Protecting the Emotional Life of Boys (Ballantine Books, 2000).
13. John Gray, Men are from Mars and Women from Venus (Harper Paperbacks, 2012).
14. Kindlon and Thompson, back cover.
15. http://davewcoachingandstorytelling.com/2017/01/26/lets-talk-about-my-bout-with-clinical-depression/ (26 January 2017)
16. David A. Walker StrengthsFinder Report 2.0. Gallup Inc. Page 2.
17. Neil Pasricha, The Five People Test (G.P. Putnam's and Sons, 2016), p. 252.
18. Gary Chapman, The Five Love Languages: The Secret to Love that Lasts, p. 15 (Northfield Publishers, 1995)
19. <http://davewcoachingandstorytelling.com/2016/07/01/blog-02/> (1 July 2016).
20. Tom Rath, Eat, Move, Sleep (Missionday, 2013).
21. <http://davewcoachingandstorytelling.com/2017/03/12/eating-healthy-does-not-have-to-taste-like-st/> (12 March 2017).
22. Clean Sweep Program. Copyright 2005 by Coach U. Inc www.coachu.com.
23. <http://davewcoachingandstorytelling.com/2017/08/24/who-are-you-the-unique-you-the-authentic-you-how-well-do-you-know-you-sharing-my-top-10-ways-that-i-got-to-know-myself-better/> (24 August 2017).
24. REACH Communications Consulting Inc., www.REACHCC.com.
25. 360 Reach TM Data Analysis and Summary report for the brand called: Dave Walker. P. 6.

26. 360 Reach TM Data Analysis and Summary report for the brand called: Dave Walker. P. 8.
27. 16 Personalities Report. NERIS Analytics Limited.
28. <http://davewcoachingandstorytelling.com/2017/01/26/lets-talk-about-my-bout-with-clinical-depression/> (26 January 2017).
29. <www.davewcoachingandstorytelling.com/MotivationalSpeaker>.
30. The COACH U Personal and Corporate Coach Training Handbook. Coach U, Inc. p. 47.
31. Travis Bradberry and Jean Greaves, Emotional Intelligence 2.0, p. 2 (Talentsmart,2009).
32. Bradberry and Greaves, p. 15.
33. <https://wellbodymindheartspirit.com/2012/06/15/the-12-symptoms-of-spiritual-awakening/> (15 June 2012).
34. Gray, p. 98.
35. <http://davewcoachingandstorytelling.com/2016/10/01/blog-05/> (1 October 2016).
36. Chapman, p. 30.
37. Research on Marriage & Divorce, American Psychological Association. <http://www.apa.org/topics/divorce/>
38. StrengthsFinder Report 2.0. Gallup Inc. Page 4.
39. PCSI – Personal Coaching Styles Inventory. Corporate Coach U International, p. 5.
40. PCSI – Personal Coaching Styles Inventory. Corporate Coach U International, p. 5.
41. PCSI – Personal Coaching Styles Inventory. Corporate Coach U International, p. 5.
42. StrengthsFinder Report 2.0. Gallup Inc., p. 7.
43. StrengthsFinder Report 2.0. Gallup Inc., p. 5.
44. The Coach U Personal Development Workbook and Guide. Coach U, Inc., p. xii.
45. <http://hughculver.com/what-tony-robbins-antarctica-and-my-dog-taught-me-about-getting-started/>.
46. The Coach U Personal Development Workbook and Guide. Coach U, Inc. Page. xii.
47. See GRIT: The Power of Passion and Perseverance, by Angela Duckworth (Vermillion 2017).
48. Randy Paterson, How to Be Miserable: 40 Strategies You Already Use (New Harbinger Publications 2016).
49. Paterson, p. 115.
50. Paterson, p. 17.

www.ingramcontent.com/pod-product-compliance
Lightning Source LLC
Chambersburg PA
CBHW070059120526
44589CB00033B/711